THE HIGHLY
PROFITABLE
ACCOUNTANT

**Take Control of Your Practice,
Make More Money and
Get Your Life Back**

Rudi Jansen

Table of Contents

Introduction: To Your Freedom

When I started in my accounting studies, my real reason, my real 'Why', could be summed up in one single word.

Freedom.

I wanted freedom.

And I knew that if I studied to become a chartered accountant, got a great job and eventually partnership, I would be well on my way to that goal.

Or that was what I thought.

Reality turned out to be slightly different.

I studied hard, all of that studying done on a part-time basis from day one, passing every single exam over all those years, until the final results of those board exams came out and I very proudly earned myself that piece of paper that said I was a chartered accountant.

In my exuberance on that day, there was one thought loud and clear in my head:

'I made it! I am on my way to freedom!'

I had achieved my dream.

Or had I?

After my initial excitement had died down, I looked around me and realised that 'freedom' wasn't anywhere to be found.

Yes, I had a high paying job. But *time* — that was something of which I had very little.

Money has a nasty habit. The more I earned, the more I spent (at the time). Which really left my net result at essentially the same point — poor, and therefore not 'free'.

Despite what I had hoped for, despite all my hard work, I had not achieved freedom, and it was still far out of my reach.

But here's the thing. Freedom *is* totally and utterly possible for any Accountancy Partner who has his or her own practice. Absolutely. Both freedom of money as well as freedom of time.

And in the pages that follow, you will learn the exact path you can take to get there.

This book is dedicated to your freedom... if you choose it.

Come and join me on this amazing adventure!

Rudi Jansen
You can reach me on *rudi@accoa.co.uk*.

Part One:
The Foundations

1. WHERE IT ALL STARTED

It was 6.10pm on a Thursday afternoon.

It was grey and raining in London that evening. I hadn't seen Phil in about 7 months. Because I was in the area, I called him up and we arranged to go for dinner at a Nando's restaurant for a catch-up.

Phil had owned his own accountancy practice for the last 9 years, and it seemed pretty successful. That Audi A6 he was driving was not exactly the cheapest car on the road. But, as in many things in life, appearances are not always what they seem.

Phil and I had a lot in common. We both qualified as chartered accountants. We both had young families.

But a few years after I qualified, my journey took me on a detour far from Phil's.

You see, I'd always had a very deep question in my psyche: "What was it that got successful business owners to be successful?" And so, in order to truly discover the answer to that question, I left the world of accountancy behind to start up as a business coach.

In order to excel as a business coach, over the years my journey has taken me all over the world, studying with some of the best mentors in order to rise to the top. And so it happened that very quietly I became one of the top business coaches in the world when it came to the results I would get with my clients.

At one stage I was even training other coaches worldwide on the systems I was using, which meant I really got to see where a lot of business coaches go wrong. I saw the good ones. I saw the bad ones. And I mentored them in how to take their game — and the game of their clients — to the next level. We tweaked the systems they were following with their clients (or rather... not following) as well as their own mindsets and fears — which hindered their own results and in turn their clients' results.

It was unusual of Phil to be late. But at about 6.30pm, a bedraggled and wet figure burst through the door from the poor weather outside. Phil was absolutely drenched. He'd decided to take a walk from his office, but the clouds opened in a torrential way and caught him by surprise with no umbrella.

I loved Phil's sense of humour — somehow he could always find something funny in almost everything. We placed our order, got a drink and had a good old catch-up.

Naturally, our conversation started drifting towards business. It was a topic we both loved.

Suddenly, Phil sat back and said, 'Rudi, I want to tell you something I have probably never said to anyone else before...'

Phil wasn't the first person in my life to say that to me. In the work I do, I hear it a lot. But it caught me off-guard nonetheless — Phil wasn't a client. Phil was a friend!

I sat waiting and after a while Phil started talking.

'Rudi, you know what... this feels strange to say, but I feel like a prisoner.

'I have my own practice. It is doing well. But there always seems to be all kinds of challenges. The reason I was late tonight is because there was a last-minute job that needed finishing for a client who is coming in tomorrow morning... and it only *just* landed on my desk.

'I don't feel like my team is pulling in the same direction as me. We are all very busy, but productivity isn't anywhere as good as I think it should be. I am working long hours, including weekends. Yet I am still concerned about the cash flow to pay the wages.

'We grow the practice mainly through recommendations and word-of-mouth. But we could really do with a good stream of new clients.

'And although I try not to take this home, it follows me everywhere. It is causing pressure in my home life and in my relationship. I don't really get to see my kids grow up, and they grow *fast*. I don't have time for hobbies or even to simply relax and enjoy life. Even when we go on holiday, I'm still plugged in. I don't ever have proper downtime.

'I've now had this practice for 9 years already. And it hasn't gotten any easier. I feel like I'm on a treadmill at its top speed and I don't know how to get off it. Sure, I've read the books. I've taken the courses. But I'm still on this treadmill.

'I'm still fully, 100% stuck in this prison.'

A silence followed for what seemed like an eternity.

And then Phil said, 'Rudi... you talk a lot about freedom in your business and about your clients who have gotten there in their own businesses...

'So how do I get to freedom from where I am?' Phil asked.

As Phil was talking, my mind was whirring and clicking at a rate of knots.

Up to that point, I had specialised — and was quite good — as a generalist Master Business Coach. Which means that over the years I had designed a number of fairly simple, straightforward systems that business owners could implement to move them step-by-step towards the results they wanted. And I had a great process for getting them to actually implement those steps.

Sitting next to Phil in Nando's, I realised that I had come from the world of accountancy, same as him. I left it behind and went into the wider world to find answers on how to create a successful business which gave the business owner freedom and choice.

At that moment, something clicked in my head.

It was that evening in Nando's that I made a decision to specialise exclusively in working only with partners who have their own accountancy practices.

It was time for me to complete the circle.

After a few moments I looked Phil squarely in the eyes and said, 'Phil, I have an idea. Will you be my guinea pig? I won't charge you anything in working with you, but I need feedback as we go through this process. I will help and support you, just as I would with any of my other clients.

But if you don't bring everything you've got to the party, I won't be able to help you. Can you promise me that?'

Phil and I shook on it, and that's when I began my journey working with Accountancy Partners to help them not only transform their practices into highly profitable organisations, but also organisations that in turn transformed their lives.

In short, I helped them achieve freedom.

Phil agreed, and that first experiment — with him as my guinea pig — bore the foundations of a process which I refined over the next year. A process that got partners to start turning their practices around to become much more profitable and to have much more free time — if that was what they wanted.

This book is about Phil, and many of my other accountant clients, and their journey to freedom. Their journey to build a practice that to a large degree could work without them, yet still give them great profits and cash flow and at the same time give them back their time... and, in a sense, their lives.

If you are at all interested in a life of choice and freedom, then I invite you on this journey with me and Phil (and a lot of my other clients, all accountants just like you) to discover how you too can create a world of choice and freedom.

2. WHERE AM I?

On our first coaching call, Phil was very excited. I could hear that he was completely re-energised.

He was ready... almost.

I could tell that he had thought a lot about the process we were about to start, but what he really wanted to cover during our call was the 101 fires he was fighting at the moment.

Which was fine, but I had to stop him in his tracks. Before we embark on a 10,000-mile journey, we first want to ensure that our car has been serviced and that the petrol tank is full.

As exciting as it was, before we started the journey there were a few absolutely key fundamentals that had to be covered and that Phil had to get to grips with. If he did not, chances were really good that we would never get to our destination!

And so our education started.

'Phil, something you have to understand is that there are two ladders. One is called "The Ladder of the Treadmill". The other is called "The Ladder of Freedom".'

Listening to this, Phil realised — he was on *the wrong ladder*.

The Ladder of the Treadmill

The steps that make up the Ladder of the Treadmill are as follows:

That's, from bottom to top, School... Employee... Self-Employed... Master of Specialism.

Somebody — perhaps a parent or a teacher — at some point in your life tells you that in order to have a great life and be successful, there is a pathway to follow.

A ladder to climb.

You go to school, you work hard, you pass your tests with flying colours... all to ensure that you can get yourself into a good university. Then you go to university and you work hard to ensure you get good grades so you can find a good job.

You find a 'good' job where you work hard and apply yourself. You continue working hard and eventually you work your way up to becoming a partner or starting your own practice.

You then focus on the continued mastering of your chosen specialism so you can get better and better at it, until you arrive at the pinnacle of your career.

You earn good money. You know your subject matter very well — after all, you've spent years on CPD to get to this point. You are a 'Master of Specialism'.

Congratulations. You're at the top.

You've made it... or have you?

The problem with this approach is that you've painted yourself into a corner.

As much as you are a Master of Specialism, you only earn money when you exchange your time for the delivery of that specialism. If you decide to go on holiday for six months, whoever is employing you (or you yourself) will have a real problem replacing the income you were generating.

And because you are a Master of Specialism, if you happen to have your own practice (or are the Managing Partner in a multi-partner practice), then you unfortunately also have all these other hassles on your shoulders which, most irritatingly, are all a part of running a business. Most of which you've not really had any proper training for. Which only increases the time you need to be a Master of Specialism.

Finding the right people is a struggle, not to mention motivating them — and then keeping them. Credit control has never been your strong point because you are such a nice person. Workflow and productivity isn't really something you track — and besides, everybody is too busy. You are working in and thinking about the practice about 60 hours a week, which you wish you weren't doing, but 'you gotta do what you gotta do'. Referrals are okay, but marketing? Oh, how you hate that word! Because that is a black hole into which a lot of money has been thrown over the years, and with very little to show for it.

And the reality is that you've hit a glass ceiling. You don't know how to get through it, and going back is not really an option for you.

So you are stuck at this plateau.

Things aren't getting much better. But they're also not getting much worse.

You're at the Okay Plateau. You are treading water. It is comfortable enough. You're making a living. You've gotten used to what you have. It is okay.

And you could stay there... forever.

But there is another way...

Freedom is an interesting thing.

Some of the elements that create freedom are:

1. Enough money
2. Enough time.

You see, in life, money is one thing. But the most important thing? That is time!

Time to live.

Time to see your kids growing up.

Time to enjoy your life.

Time to do the things that give you a real buzz.

Time to grow as a human being.

Time to practice your hobbies.

Time to make a significant difference.

So a great question to ask yourself is, 'How much time do I have left?'

The average life expectancy in the UK for males is 79 years. Females, 81 years. Subtract your current age from the appropriate number above. The answer you get is roughly how many years you have left on this earth. Depending on your current age, your remaining years may be quite a few still... or perhaps not so many.

Either way, the reality is that time is the one thing that you *cannot squander*. When it is gone, it is gone forever. No turning back the clock.

Staying on that path of hard work on autopilot is easy. In fact, I often say that working hard is the lazy man's way. Why?

Because it requires no thinking. You just keep going.

But pausing, taking stock, doing things differently in order to obtain different results — *that* is hard work. The good news? The hard work is only in the beginning. Once it is implemented, you can actually enjoy, really, truly enjoy, your life.

So let's take a look at a different ladder.

The Ladder of Freedom

The steps that make up the Ladder of Freedom are as follows:

That's, from bottom to top, School... Employee... Self-Employed... Business Owner... Investor.

Somebody — perhaps a parent or a teacher — at some point in your life tells you that in order to have a great life and be successful, there is a pathway to follow.

A ladder to climb.

You go to school, you work hard, you pass your tests with flying colours... all to ensure that you can get yourself into university. Then you go to university and you work hard to ensure you get good grades so you can find a good job.

You find a 'good' job where you work hard and apply yourself.

This is the E step of the ladder and it stands for 'Employee'.

At some point we become an employee who learns to do a trade with their hands. Whether as a plumber or a bookkeeper, we work with our hands in whichever way we've been trained.

Then one day, you wake up and decide that you have had enough of working for someone — you can do a much better job yourself. So you become Self-Employed. Or perhaps you really enjoy working with your boss, so you go into partnership with him or her.

The main similarity between E and SE is that in both cases you are the one with your hands out doing your art.

The next jump on this ladder is where the differences start.

These differences are initially very subtle — so subtle, in fact, that most people completely miss them.

This is the jump to BO — Business Owner. This is the step that most of my clients are on.

At BO, we tie your hands behind your back and we say, 'Okay — now run this business the same *or better* than you did before.' And whilst we tie your hands behind your back, you are kicking and screaming, shouting 'No, no, let me go, I need my hands... no, no, set me free!'

And we say, 'When you know how to do this with your hands tied firmly behind your back — *that* is when you will truly be free!'

This is a very different skill set to anything you've learnt before. To be successful on the BO step (and get to the point where you are about to jump onto the I step), you will have mastered two major skills. You will have mastered 1) having the right team; and 2) having the right systems upon which that team relies.

When you get to the point where you've totally embodied this learning — and you have put the right team in place as well as the right systems for that team — that is the point where you finally get to *freedom*. You will have built yourself a great profitable business with a team running it for you.

Which means you are ready to make the jump onto the I step — Investor.

That is an interesting place to be in. It is a place where you have choice. It is also the place where you really start playing *Monopoly*.

Over the years I've only had one client, Raymond, who, after making this jump, then decided to spend most of his time purely on enjoying his remaining years. But Raymond made a conscious decision. We started working together when he was in his early 60s. His wife of almost 40 years had tragically passed away the previous year from cancer. He knew that retirement was only a few years away and he wanted his young son, Chris, to take over the business. In that process, not only was Chris trained up within a couple of years on how to run a multimillion-pound business very effectively — and very profitably — but at the same time, Chris was moved onto the I step, too. Chris is still involved in this business, but Raymond has focused on enjoying his last years and has great holidays travelling the world with his new wife.

But all my other clients who have made this jump — well, they all started playing real-life *Monopoly*. Because they have learnt the rules of the game. They have embodied how it all works. And once you know how to 'ride the bicycle', well, then you can climb on pretty much any bicycle and off you go. So they either start new businesses or they acquire businesses and transform them — and those businesses are not limited to accountancy practices.

What a fantastic place to be in.

So the questions you have to ask yourself are:

1.   On which ladder am I?
2.   On which ladder do I want to be?
3.   On which step of the ladder am I spending most of my time?
4.   If I am on the SE step, how close am I to reaching BO?

Once you get yourself onto the I step, you will have real freedom. Freedom of both money and time, so you can enjoy your life and do the things you really want to do.

But right now you are on a step of the ladder, and the question to ask is...

'Why do I choose to stay where I am?'

As we went through this conversation, Phil realised that he had been on the wrong ladder. He was on the Ladder of the Treadmill. And it was costing him dearly. Both in money and, more importantly, in time. It was costing him the option of living a life of choice.

He realised that on the Ladder of Freedom, he was definitely stuck on the SE step. And if he had to estimate how close he was to the BO step, he said that he wasn't even halfway there.

But as Phil said, 'Rudi... for the first time, I really see a light at the end of the tunnel. True, I don't quite know how to get there yet, but I am going to trust you and your process. What is the next step?'

3. WHERE AM I GOING?

Some fundamentals in life are so simple that they are really easy to forget.

As easy as forgetting to put eggs into the cake mix, to put air into the tyres, to look for oncoming cars when crossing the road...

Some fundamentals are so incredibly obvious. And yet, sometimes because they are so incredibly obvious, we forget them.

And that costs us dearly!

Phil's question, 'Rudi, you've mentioned some fundamentals that we need to cover before we get into the "real" stuff. What are you talking about?'

'Phil,' I said, 'before I go on holiday, I want to be 100% certain that I have programmed my Satellite Navigation System and that I'm clear on where I am going, because that way I am fairly certain I am going to get there.'

So I asked Phil if he was 100% clear on what he wanted for:

1. His personal life
2. His practice

The answer was similar to hundreds I've heard over the years. He said, 'Well, Rudi, I guess I haven't really thought about it. I have a rough idea where I want to go. I want to build a great business which is respected in my community.'

Now that might sound like a fair answer.

But actually, it is an extremely weak answer.

That's a bit like getting into your car and programming into your Satellite Navigation System that you are 'going north'.

As Alice says to the Cheshire Cat in Lewis Carroll's *Alice's Adventures in Wonderland*, 'Would you tell me, please, which way I ought to go from here?'

'That depends a good deal on where you want to get to,' said the Cat.

'I don't much care where —' said Alice.

'Then it doesn't matter which way you go,' said the Cat.

So I started working with Phil on two very important steps to gain *extreme* clarity.

Step 1: What do you want for your personal life?

Step 2: What business do we need to build to give you the life you really want?

The two steps outlined in this chapter are a *huge* and extremely *vital* key to find your direction.

I know that most people are so eager to learn the tactics and the techniques that this is the part where they start scanning ahead to the chapters on 'How to...' So if your brain is going, 'Ah, I already know this, I'll come back to it another day because I *really* want to get to the "real" stuff later in this book,' then now is the time to sit your brain down, and have a very good heart-to-brain conversation.

'Brain — I really do appreciate your incredible eagerness to get to the good stuff. Even though you may not realise it yet, the content we're about to cover in this chapter — without this content, the "good" stuff later in the book are just pieces of flotsam floating around in a sea with nothing that really connects it. And it doesn't work anywhere near as well as it should be doing.

'So Brain, let's linger here a little longer and delve deep into this chapter. Because the author says it is *really* important, so if you'll humour me, let's go with the flow — the later chapters are still going to be there *later*.

'For now, let's put our focus here...'

Step 1: What Do You Want For Your Personal Life?

This step is important because everyone wants to have lived a life that at the end of the day they can go, 'Wow...that was an absolutely amazing experience. I loved *every single* moment of it.'

In order to get that kind of outcome, it is important that you sit down and to some extent put reality as you know it aside and ask yourself a question...

'If I had a magic wand in my hand, what would I *really* want for my personal life?'

Because once we're clear on that, then we can start working on the next step, which is 'What kind of practice do you need to build to give you the personal life you really really want?'

This step was an interesting one for me. For many years my wife and I would sit down once a year, typically the week after Christmas, and decide what we wanted, especially for the following year. And often during that process I'd come up with goals that deep down I didn't really feel connected with. Yes, they were goals, targets... but somehow I just wasn't connecting.

I remember one year I picked a goal: to fly in a private jet on a 60-day journey travelling the world. Yes, sure, that is a nice goal. But anyone who knows me will realise that status and ego just isn't on my radar. I respect that others have it, but for me, it is gobbledygook and it simply doesn't make any sense. So this goal, even though I had picked it, wasn't truly connected to who I am.

And that was when a mentor of mine at the time showed me a simple but very powerful step that completely transformed how I could not only decide about what I really wanted, but also ensure that I actually *connected* to what I wanted.

Step 1 starts with a simple spreadsheet with a few columns. Column 1 is a list of all the things I *don't* want in my world.

Create a list of categories for your life. Here are some examples.

1. Business/Career
2. Finance
3. Personal Growth
4. Health
5. Family/Friends
6. Romance
7. Fun/Recreation
8. Physical Environment

Then under each category list the things you *don't* want in your life.

Take your time with this. It is important!

After you've completed that list, in the column to the right of that turn each of those negatives into positives.

Let's say in Column 1 under the category of Business/Career one of my items is, 'I don't want to work 60 hours per week' — then Column 2 becomes, 'I work in this business a maximum of 35 hours per week.'

Column 1 under the category of Finance is, 'I don't want to be earning £50k per year' — Column 2 becomes, 'I am earning more than £150k per year from this business.'

Column 1 under the category of Family/Friends is, 'I don't want to be spending only one quality day a week with my family' — Column 2 becomes, 'I have at least two quality days a week with my family and one quality day a week for myself and my hobbies.'

Obviously these lists are going to be very personal to yourself. But by doing it in this format, you are suddenly connecting all your *Don't Want*s to your *Do Want*s.

Once you've completed Column 1 and Column 2 and there is nothing left over anymore, then you start creating Column 3.

Column 3 is written as a story.

Imagine that it is the following December. You are walking down the street on the righthand pavement. On the opposite side of the street you see an old friend, so you cross the road to catch up with him. And as you meet up, you realise that your friend is actually an older you. *(Sceptics... stay with me.)* You greet each other and you can see the excitement in his/her eyes as he/she tells you about the amazing last 12 to 18 months.

And this Future You tells the current you all your positive phrases from Column 2 as if it had already happened in a story format.

Here are some examples illustrated from the points above.

Future You says, 'Things have really changed and it is so exciting. Now you are only working 35 hours a week within the business; there is an amazing team and systems in place. Things have changed so much that during this past year you've easily taken £150k out of the business — something that you had thought was completely impossible before. And to top it off, you're spending two days a week with the family in quality time as well as an extra day on hobbies and yourself.'

He is shaking his head. He is so excited and says that he still can't believe it.

You are really excited for him that all these things have already happened. You thank him/her for sharing this with you. You give each other a goodbye hug and off you go.

Ensure that every sentence and image in this story is in the positive (so not 'I don't want to work 60 hours'), because the subconscious brain does not recognise *don't* or *not* — instead it will only give you the leftover point in the sentence structure. The same way as when I say, *Don't imagine a blue elephant.* Your brain has to see the blue elephant before it can elect to make it disappear. Instead of 'Don't want to work 60 hours,' state the positive 'I do want to work 35 hours.'

Why does this work?

Well, I don't really know. And to be honest — I don't really care.

It is the same as when I say, *Imagine two blue elephants flying through the sky.* In your mind's eye, you can see that, even though we all know it isn't real. But your subconscious mind is unable to determine reality from fantasy, as long as you simply imagine it. And the subconscious mind at some level takes over and will always deliver to you that which it thinks is what you want your reality to be.

So Step 1: get complete clarity about what you actually want for your personal life. Once you've done that, we can start with Step 2. Step 2 is all about gaining clarity on what you want your accountancy practice to look like.

Step 2: Let's Create the Strategic Plan for Your Practice So That We Can Build You the Business You Really Want, Which in Turn Will Give You the Life You Discovered You Really Wanted in Step 1!

Now that you have clarity on what it is that you want for your personal life, the next step is to decide what it is that you need to build that will give you that life.

Remember: the minutes, the hours, the days, the years are zipping by at a fast rate. No time to waste.

The first time I met up with Jonathan, I realised that by all accounts he had already created a very successful practice, and definitely one of the most profitable ones I had ever seen. Jonathan was already in his late 60s, and as a young man he took over the practice from his father. So it would be fair to say that he had literally been in this game all his life. Over the years, Jonathan had met up with his fair share of consultants and business coaches, and he had done and seen more than his fair share of 'strategic plans'.

Just after we had spoken for the first time on the phone, Jonathan said, 'Rudi, I had heard about you from someone else whom I very much admire, and he is a client of yours, so I thought I might as well give it a try.'

He then proceeded to tell me about a plan for his business that he'd scribbled down and that he would forward to me via email. What I received truly was a rambling of scribbles covering six pages. But at the end of the six pages, neither I nor Jonathan were any clearer on what in the world he needed to build or how in the world he was going to do it.

So I promised Jonathan that I'd take him through a process that will blow his mind. A process that on the face of it seems really very simple.

And it is.

Jonathan looked sceptical, to say the least. But to his credit, he jumped in and gave it a go. Which is all I would ask of anybody.

And at the end of that process, Jonathan looked up, stared at me over his glasses, pushed himself back in his chair and said, 'Rudi — you did say that this would blow my mind. When we started this morning, I had no real clear idea of where we were going and how to get there. And now, only a few hours later, I will agree with you — this process *has* blown my mind! On a single A4 page is a clear, common goal as well as the exact roadmap to get us there. I am impressed."

The process I am about to describe to you is the exact same process I took Jonathan through.

To make the next part of this chapter easier to understand, I'd recommend that you download the worksheet that accompanies this process from www.accoa.co.uk/thehighlyprofitableaccountantworksheets

On the sheet, I want you to write down the name of your organisation and today's date. Keep in mind, the name on the document is *not* your name. It is the name of the company. This is the strategic plan for the business.

The next section is a SWOTT analysis — Strengths, Weaknesses, Opportunities, Threats and Trends. This is limited to five answers for each of those sections. At the end of the day this is also a big focusing exercise. So if you have more than five answers for a section, write them all down separately and then pick the biggest five.

The next section covers your Big, Hairy, Audacious Goal (your BHAG). Pick a time period 10 years from today.

Read closely: here is a common mistake that needs to be avoided.

The answer to the question 'What is our BHAG?' can be arrived at in one of two ways. The first is when we pretend that we are typical, logical, analytical accountants. We start with 'This is where I am now, and if I increase incrementally by 10% per year for the next 10 years, then in 10 years where I'll end up is X...'

The second method is much more powerful...

If you and I were to sit around a table ten years from today, my goal is to have you sitting there with a huge, happy grin on your face because over the last 10 years you've had a magic wand in your hand and you've created this amazing business which is giving you an absolutely incredible lifestyle — the life of your dreams. With this magic wand in your hand (tip: the answer here comes from a dream space, not a logical space!!!) paint me a picture. But give this to me specifically in terms of:

1. 10 years from now, in today's terms, what is your turnover for that year?
2. What is your net profit before partner's drawings in that year?
3. How many staff do you have in that year?
4. How many hours per week on average do you work in that year?
5. How many weeks of holidays have you taken in that year?

Keep in mind that the answers need to end up putting an excited, happy grin on your face when you think about it.

Also keep in mind the three zones where your answers could lie:

Zone 1: The Yawn Zone
Zone 2: The Butterfly Zone
Zone 3: The Dead Zone.

Zone 1: If your current turnover is £500,000 and you say to me, 'Rudi, in 10 years I'd like that to be at £550,000"… this is the Yawn Zone. This book, and true freedom, is meant for big thinkers!

Zone 2: The Butterfly Zone is the 'on the edge' zone. This is the answer you think of where your stomach churns a little and you go, 'Ooh… not so sure, but wow — if we did that, that would be really exciting!!!'

Zone 3: Your current turnover is £500,000 and you say to me that in 10 years' time you want to be turning over £30 million. Both you and I know that your entire system is in complete disbelief and that this goal is totally ridiculous for you. What happens here is that your system, your brain, goes into shut-down mode. It says, 'Yes, I've picked that as a goal, but that is just never, ever going to happen.'

The answer you arrive at for your BHAG needs to be in Zone 2, the Butterfly Zone.

There is an interesting phenomenon that often happens with BHAG.

On Day 1 when it is chosen, it is usually at the top end of the Butterfly Zone. And normally within a period of about 18 to 24 months, people start saying, 'Well, it seemed almost impossible on Day 1, but now we are making really big strides towards that. A few of the things we mentioned in our BHAG on Day 1 have already been achieved and that goal doesn't seem so far off anymore...'

The next step on the Strategic Planning Spreadsheet is to work backwards.

Trust the process.

Right underneath the BHAG we decide the five main focus areas that we need to focus our energy on during years 8, 9 and 10 in order for us to achieve our BHAG.

In the next column we are working on a timeline of three years from now.

What do we want our turnover to be, our profits, and in which geographic market places do we want to be?

Below that, fill in the five main areas we need to focus on during the 12 months before the year-three point that will help us achieve our three-year goal. These five things very well may be a copy-and-paste exercise of the previous five focus areas, or it may be slightly different.

The next column is one year from now. What do we want our turnover to be and our profits? Are there any other numbers we specifically want to target, e.g. debtors' days/WIP days, etc.

Below that, fill in the five main areas we need to focus on during the next 12 months. Again, these five things very well may be a copy-and-paste exercise of the previous five focus areas — but you'll probably start finding that by this stage, you'll want to put a bit more detail into those areas.

Example: before it may have been 'Retain effective marketing'. Now it may be 'Develop and implement a written-down Tactical Marketing Plan'.

Then we repeat the same with the last column which covers the next quarter — the next three months. What do you expect your turnover and profits to be for the next three months? Any specific financial targets, e.g. debtors' days/WIP days?

And in this case we are limited to *only* three quarterly goals to work on your business.

These are linked to your annual goals, so review the five focus areas you've decided for the year and pick three of them (or elements of those) to set as your goals for the quarter.

Maximum three goals for the quarter — because *less is more*.

Some of the biggest mistakes I see that people make are:

1. Choosing too many goals;
2. Too vague;
3. Too big for a three-month period.

Be very clear, and chunk it down so that whatever you decide it is, it can be completed within a period of three months.

Laser focus. Go small.

And then we go to the last column.

Here we want to do a quick exercise to determine the values of your business. The way we do this is to start with the personal value of you and your partners. Because at the end of the day, your business is a mirror — it is a reflection of you.

So let's decide your personal values, and then based on that list, we decide the values of your business.

Start coming up with a list of things that are really important to you. This will be different for every person, but it may include concepts such as Honesty, Integrity, Fun, Family and so on. Once you've got your list of words, the next step is to go through that list and decide which ones are relevant to your business — perhaps you need to change, delete or add some more words.

Once you've completed that exercise — we fully appreciate that all of those words are important, but stay with me — if you had to highlight the top three, which ones would they be?

Tips

When you are considering your annual and quarterly goals, do refer back to your current weaknesses and ensure they are somehow or another addressed within these goals.

'So Phil, now that we've completed these exercises, what are your biggest insights?' I asked him.

'I've got complete clarity both on what I want for my personal life and how to achieve it. That was a real eye-opener for both me and my wife. Because what we really want, the dream, is to live on a yacht in the Mediterranean for six months of the year. And the Strategic Plan Worksheet has painted a picture of how to get there with a management team in charge. I have a very clear roadmap now,' Phil said.

That brings the exercise to an end. You are now, on a single A4 page, very clear on your Strengths, Weaknesses, Opportunities, Threats and Trends. You've decided your BHAG and you've also created a clear roadmap on how to get there.

All you have to do is ensure that, each quarter, you focus on getting your three main goals completed. And at the end of the quarter you select your next three goals. It doesn't take a rocket scientist to figure out that if you stay with this process and keep implementing, before long you will be at the point where your BHAG becomes well within reach.

By completing the top two exercises — your SWOTT and your BHAG — before you start tinkering on making your practice better, you will gain incredible clarity. And that will help you with your 'Why'. You will understand *why* you could even be bothered to make changes to your practice. And after the Strategic Plan Worksheet has been completed, you will have a roadmap on exactly how to go about making the necessary changes — one step at a time.

Important Note:

The *order* in which you decide to implement the rest of the information contained within this book depends on what your quarterly goals are.

This *will* vary from one practice to another.

It is important to get this right and prioritise the right goals — otherwise you will end up wasting a lot of energy and time focusing on the wrong goals at the wrong time, which will only lead to unnecessary frustrations.

4. USING MY MIND'S EYE

'Phil, I want you to pay close attention to this,' I said. 'I want to share with you one of the most powerful tools that you will ever have in your arsenal.'

He looked intrigued.

I said, 'Let's do a quick exercise first.

'Imagine that you are in your kitchen. You pick up a lemon. You can feel the rough texture of the lemon on your skin. You can feel its temperature. You can feel the weight of it in your hand. You get a faint smell of it in your nose as you breathe. You see its bright yellow colour. In your other hand you pick up a knife and you put the lemon down on a cutting board. Slowly and carefully you start slicing through the lemon. You can hear the knife slicing the lemon and you can smell the citrus. As you slice more, you see the juice running onto the cutting board. The two halves fall open as you put the knife down — you hear the clang of metal on the table.

'You pick up one half of the lemon and you raise it above your head. You stretch your head back and open your mouth and slowly start squeezing on the lemon, feeling the pressure in your fingers. And slowly a drop of juice forms at the bottom of the lemon, it gets bigger and eventually it starts a slow fall towards your outstretched tongue. The lemon juice falls onto your tongue and you can taste the sourness of it in your mouth.

'Okay — let's leave the kitchen and come back to where you are right now.

'So Phil, tell me what happened as we were going through that story.'

'Well,' Phil said, 'I could really see, smell, feel and hear the lemon. All my senses felt engaged. And at the end I was salivating.'

So, if you did this exercise as you read, despite the fact that there is probably not a lemon anywhere in actual sight, you've used your mind's eye to create an image of your own choosing (well, mine in this case to illustrate the point) and that image has had a physical impact on your body.

This phenomenon is very well known — in fact, all of us are using our mind's eye all the time.

Let's take a look at the world of sports where the mind's eye and mental imagery is constantly used by top athletes and Olympians alike.

Golfer Jack Nicklaus used mental imagery for every shot. In describing how he imagined his performance, he wrote:

> *I never hit a shot even in practice without having a sharp in-focus picture of it in my head. It's like a colour movie. First, I 'see' the ball where I want it to finish, nice and white and sitting up high on the bright green grass. Then the scene quickly changes, and I 'see' the ball going there: its path, trajectory, and shape, even its behaviour on landing. Then there's a sort of fade-out, and the next scene shows me making the kind of swing that will turn the previous images into reality and only at the end of this short private Hollywood spectacular do I select a club and step up to the ball.*

Upfront warning to all sceptics:

As you read through the remainder of this chapter and you perhaps start to think to yourself that this is all a bit weird and Rudi has clearly lost it, keep in mind that I am merely sharing some of my own as well as others' experiences. At the end of this chapter you are absolutely welcome to agree or disagree. Keep reading, and try to keep an open mind. The rest of the book is much more grounded in reality as you know it.

Using your mind's eye to imagine the world you want to achieve (as if it has already been achieved) is one of the most powerful and potent tools you will ever come across!

I recall the first time I learnt this knowledge and started playing around with it — within weeks things were starting to happen that really should not have happened. The result was that I sat up and said to myself, 'Hang on... I have absolutely no idea what is happening here, but I can see the results. So despite the fact that I have absolutely no understanding of how this works, since it is getting me the results I want, I should keep on doing it.'

At the time I lived in Johannesburg in South Africa, and my mother was living in a city called Durban about 400 miles away. She had problems with her health and wasn't particularly well at the time. I strongly felt the need to go and visit her to give her some moral support, but because I was doing my articles at an accountancy firm at the time, my income was quite meagre, to say the least. I simply didn't have a lot of cash, so in order to save money, I hatched a plan whereby I would travel down on a Friday by coach (a whole day's journey), visit for the weekend and then travel back again on Monday.

When I came across this knowledge I'm about to share with you, initially I was a complete non-believer, a true sceptic. But I thought to myself that I had absolutely nothing to lose, so why not give it a try?

I put the process in place because it takes only ten minutes per day. In the same way as Jack Nicklaus described his mental imagery, I created a mental video which I played in my mind's eye. In the video I imagined in great detail that I had just returned from the weekend of visiting my mother. I had flown there, flown back and was very excited that I had been able to save lots of time by flying.

I had no money, so it was obviously very clear to me that this "video" I was playing in my mind's eye on a daily basis was complete rubbish, but I still persisted. Ten minutes *every day* playing the video as if it had *already happened*. Feeling the feelings as if I had already achieved it.

Three weeks after I started playing the mind's-eye video on a daily basis, I was on a big contract helping a large charity client develop a very intricate budget spreadsheet with lots of variables and all kinds of formulas in it which they needed in order to make a huge presentation to acquire funding for the following year.

I went to the partner at the practice and put in leave for the Friday and the Monday explaining that my mom wasn't very well and that I had to go and see her. My leave was granted.

The following day, walking into the client's office, the CEO called me in for an urgent meeting. She had heard about my leave and she had a proposal for me. Because of the immense time pressure on getting the budget completed, they couldn't afford to lose me for two whole days.

If they were to pay for a return flight ticket for me, would I work until Friday evening, fly to Durban and then fly back again on Sunday evening in order to be back at work again Monday morning?

Obviously it made complete logical sense for me to agree!

But I walked out of the office having to pinch myself... what just happened there?

To this day, I don't know — and quite frankly, I don't care.

Of course — we could say it was 'coincidence.' And that is the whole point. When you practice this kind of metal imagery on a consistent basis, all kinds of 'coincidences' consistently start happening. Doors that you did not even realised where there, start opening. You start meeting people who just happen to have the exact solutions you are seeking. Opportunities arrive out of nowhere.

Here is my meagre attempt at an explanation of how the mind's eye works (and if you really are interested, a lot of scientific research has gone into this topic and much has been written about it).

Each of us human beings is like a magnet and we have an electromagnetic forcefield around us.

With our conscious minds we have the ability to programme this magnetic field of ours. By deciding consciously what video we wish to play (remember, in Step 1 we created our video), we then run that video through our heads for ten minutes at least once every single day. Typically, within around 90 days, you will start noticing things happen. Coincidences. Bumping into the right people. Doors opening where you didn't even realise they existed. Strange things start happening. And over time, irrelevant of your current reality, this video starts becoming reality.

It is like having a glass of water and next to it a small bottle of red ink with a dropper. Each day we put one drop of red ink into the glass. What happens? Initially, nothing happens. But you keep repeating this exercise day after day, and eventually the water will turn completely red.

On the other hand, what is the video that most people run through their minds on a consistent basis? Well — they turn themselves into victims. 'Life is tough.' 'I just can't find the right clients.' 'I can't find the right people.' 'We're in a recession.' 'There are terrorists everywhere.' 'Don't speak to strangers.' And on and on the negativity goes.

So if that is the video you are subconsciously programming into your mind's eye on a daily basis, guess what types of coincidences are going to start happening to you? Guess what that magnet draws to itself?

To this day I am still using this process. Why in the world would I not? Either I programme my own magnetic field with what I want, or I feed it with unnecessary negativity.

The seminal book on this subject (and there are a lot), is *Mind Power Into The 21st Century* by John Kehoe. I encourage you to read it for more information.

The keys to get your mind's eye to work for you:

1. Decide the story your video tells, which you determined in the previous chapter.
2. Develop a daily routine where you can sit quietly for 10 minutes completely undisturbed in a relaxed state.
3. Play the video through your head as if it has already happened.
4. Involve as many emotions as you can muster into the movie — remember the lemon!
5. Feel how excited you are at the end because of this exciting reality that has already happened in your mind.
6. When finished, open your eyes and return to your normal world.

Once a day is good, twice a day is brilliant.

Note: this doesn't work anywhere as well if you are inconsistent, if you do it for two days, do nothing for three days, do it for one day, do nothing for six days, do it for three days and so on. This wants a *daily* routine. Each and every day you keep dropping the red ink into the glass. Then the energy builds, your magnetic field gets charged with your consciously decided video. And something starts happening...

This force is *always* at play. You can choose to use it. Or you can choose to ignore it.

If you really are serious about creating the life of your dreams, then take the time to complete the steps in the previous chapter which will give you incredible clarity. Then create your video and decide a daily routine to play your video in your mind's eye. Do it regularly as if your life depends on it, because in reality — it does.

So I said to my friend, Phil, 'These are the fundamentals that we need to get into place before we start with the *real* stuff.'

Phil did have one question though.

'Rudi, this is really interesting. Does this mean I could create anything? If I could imagine it, if I could create a video in my head which I then repeat over and over, could I ultimately create anything?'

And this is what I said to him:

'Phil, as long as it results in good, then yes — ultimately you could probably imagine and therefore create almost anything. You want to improve your relationship with your partner or your children? You want an A-plus team? You want to work only two days a week? You want to travel the world? You want ten new A-plus clients? Whatever it is... if you create a short video of it as if it has already happened, and then repeat that video in your head over and over and over, day after day after day — at some point it will happen.'

Phil didn't sound too convinced, but full credit to him: he dived right in and implemented a daily routine of playing his mental video in his mind's eye.

And, extra credit to Phil — he repeated this exercise every single day.

Part Two:
The Structures

5. THE BROKEN MODEL AND HOW TO FIX IT.

The week after our discussion about the mind's eye, late on a Tuesday afternoon, I was on a phonecall with Phil about starting to implement his first set of business goals.

He sounded very frustrated.

'Rudi — I promise you I am doing this "mind's eye" thing every day. But I just don't get it. I'm working these crazy hours, my wife is really not happy. And quite frankly, I'm squashing time in for my kids over the weekend, because my mind is always on the problems here at the practice, the things that haven't been done yet, and the things we've still got to do. I feel like I'm forever playing catch-up.

'Rudi — to be honest, between you and me — I sometimes miss just having a job and working for someone else. And all these hassles could be someone else's.'

And then he laughed. Because he knew as he said it that going back wasn't truly one of the options. Going forwards and figuring it out was the only way for him.

So this was my response to him:

'Phil... let me explain it this way. It is late at night. It is raining. I rush out to my car, get in... and I realise, as I turn the key in the ignition, that my one light isn't working, my brakes are faulty and the steering wheel of the car is loose.

'Now, clearly I have a number of options here. My best option, quite frankly, is probably to get out of the car and call a taxi, or just make other plans. Another option is to start driving despite all the faults.

'Now, for argument's sake, let's say that I chose the latter option and I do indeed start driving the car. Imagine how I will be feeling as I sit there. I am going to be breaking out in a cold sweat, with a huge amount of tension and angst in my body. Constantly worried and on red alert. Not for a moment being able to switch off and relax. Constantly wishing

I was already at my destination — wanting to be in a better place because the one I'm finding myself in is an absolute drag!

'And what would I rather be doing? I'd rather stop that car, open the door and run far away!'

Now, agreed — that is a bit of an extreme example. But let's take a look at you in your practice.

Do you ever feel angst in your body? Tension? Do you ever feel that you're unable to switch off? Worried, unable to truly relax, even when you are on holiday? Wishing that your practice was in a different place than where it is?

So when I look at the feelings I have while sitting in that faulty car I'm driving... *it is pretty obvious that the reason for those negative feelings is that the car I'm driving is broken.*

And the truth is that when you are feeling similar unhappy feelings within or about your practice... *it is pretty obvious that the reason for those negative feelings is that the model you are driving your business on is — yes, you guessed it — broken!*

After I explained this to Phil, he said, 'Rudi, I totally get what you mean about the car story; that makes total sense. But I don't really get what you mean about the business analogy.'

Okay, let's put it like this.

The model your practice is built on consists of a triangle with three corners.

Let's call those three corners Team, Systems and Growth.

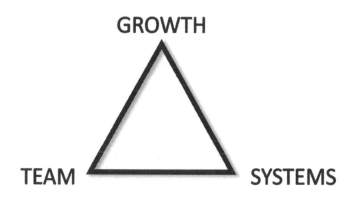

GROWTH

TEAM   SYSTEMS

On the earlier 'Ladder of Freedom' that I mentioned, in order for you to be able to make the jump completely from SE to the top of BO, the three corners on that triangle all need to be 100% complete.

If any one of those three corners is not completed, is not ticked, it will hold you trapped within your practice and stop you from making the jump onto the I step.

It is like a Formula 1 car — even a tiny little screw out of place can wreck the whole thing.

If you are serious about building a practice that:

1) Makes you money, and
2) Gives you your time back so you can actually go and enjoy your life

That means that you have to get serious about all three corners on this triangle — and you have to get all three corners just right.

It is completely and utterly possible to do.

Many others before you have done this. Just like our Olympic athletes who are going for gold, it is vital to have an accountability partner to take you through the process and keep you focused in order to get you there, and for you to be clear on what the next steps are.

So let's take a look at what each of those three corners stand for.

Team

As a business owner, you are either looking forwards, building your business, or you are looking backwards, fixing your team and their problems. But you can't be looking forwards *and* backwards at the same time.

And that is the reason why you need an A+ team behind you. Because if you are going for the Olympic gold medal, you absolutely need an A+ team behind you. It is completely okay to have a B or a C team behind you, but then you simply have to accept that you will never get to the gold (namely your Big Hairy Audacious Goal).

If you choose and if you are content with a B or a C team, that is okay — but you need to accept this and stop complaining.

When it comes to ticking this corner, under 'Team', there are four subheadings that need to be ticked.

1. Self
2. A+ Core Team
3. My Outsourced Team
4. How to Manage and Delegate to Get *Real* Results

In the next chapters we will go into more detail on what exactly each of those is, and how we go about putting those in place in your practice.

Systems

At the end of the day, to get properly onto the BO step so that you can make that final jump onto the I step, you will need a great team behind you and you will need your practice to be fully systemised.

Your great people rely on your great systems. When you have that, you will have a fantastic business — a money-making machine that will give you your life back.

"If you're too busy to build good systems, then you'll always be too busy"

Clearly you have systems in your practice. You haven't gotten to where you are without having a lot of systems in place already.

But we now want to fine-tune those systems and ensure that all of them work 100%.

In what we will be looking at, I'm going to ignore all your technical systems — the technical side of what you do. Obviously you need systems for those, and for most accountancy practices, they have those systemised already.

The main places where a lack of proper systems holds accountancy practices back are the following:

1. Systemised customer service
2. Systemised on-boarding of new clients
3. Debtors
4. WIP
5. KPIs
6. Technology

Let's take a quick look at the impact of either having, or not having, those systems:

System	If we don't have it in place	If we do have it in place
Customer service	Customers feel unloved, ad-hock touch bases. Relationship naturally declines, leaving clients more vulnerable to being poached by other firms.	Customers feel highly appreciated and loved, which leads to more referrals as well as more cross-sell opportunities and price acceptance. They're much more immune to being poached.
On-boarding system for new clients	It is a medium-rated experience for our new clients. Wasted opportunity to create a 'Wow!' which leads to less referrals and less cross-selling opportunities.	'Wow!' experience from the word 'go'. Leads to higher levels of trust and also more referrals as well as cross-selling opportunities.
Debtors	High debtors' days with lots of our cash locked up completely unnecessarily. Because we are on the back foot chasing debt, it reduces the ability in our relationship with our clients for cross-selling and also increasing fees. Can lead to cash flow problems on our side.	Our relationship with our clients is 'cleaner'. Money comes in automatically and we don't have to raise this subject with our clients which means there is no psychological barrier in the way to truly sitting down with them, listening to their challenges and therefore being able to comfortably offer them other services which would benefit them, and at the same time increase our revenue and profit levels.

WIP	Work sits on our desks far too long, creating inefficiencies on our side (which, like it or not, does go straight to the bottom line). The time I wasted making another phonecall to chase up, moving papers from this side of the desk to that corner and then again into another corner... that is time I've been unproductive and not getting work out the door. And this of course leads to write-offs. (Some firms I know *budget* for 20% write-offs per year.) So they're counting on being inefficient and at the same time have no learning process in place to rectify it for next year... this can also lead to client dissatisfaction with turnaround taking too long.	This leads to fast turnaround times. We are able to get into a situation where we create write-ons instead of write-offs. Clients are impressed with our promptness at getting their work completed and back to them.
KPIs	Two sets of KPIs: one for our team members and another for our business. When we don't have these in place (or we do, but we are drowning in data, so it isn't particularly useful and just confuses everyone), then we're not setting targets, there is no accountability and we get into a Drift Zone. Everyone is very busy, but we're not particularly achieving. Profits aren't where they're meant to be. We're working very hard, yet client retention suffers.	With this in place, everyone knows what they are aiming for. When targets are not met, we learn from it and rectify what we're doing (or on occasion we exit the wrong people!). Efficiencies shoot through the roof — and profitability with it.

Technology	Without using technology to its fullest potential, we are going much slower than we could be doing. Examples: a bit of software that can scan or automatically import a bank statement is much faster than a human manually typing; using a portal eliminates postage, paper, time spent on getting it to the post-office, being on the journey, being with the client awaiting signatures and then at some point hopefully being posted back to us.	With this in place at an optimal level, it saves time, saves money, increases speed and increases efficiency — which always has a positive impact on the bottom line. Getting things done faster also makes our clients happier.

Having those systems properly in place leads to happier clients, which leads to more referrals as well as more direct business with those same clients. You will have happier team members and, in turn, much higher productivity and profitability.

In other words...cash in your bank account.

Growth

To be fair, these relate to Systems as well, but because it is such a big field, it is better to keep it as a separate corner on our triangle. 'Systems' relate to the systems we need to make our clients (and us) happy. 'Growth' relates to systems that help us get more of those clients or those same clients to pay us more money for more value.

Under the Growth category, we have five main subheadings:

1. Tactical Marketing Plan: a written-down plan we have in place which we can execute against and hold ourselves accountable to doing. Under this section in the relevant chapter, we will look at the different strategies that you need to get involved in and how exactly you do that in a step-by-step process.
2. Sales Process: marketing has to do with getting interested parties to put up their hand and say, 'I *may* be interested in talking to you.' This is the step-by-step process of what happens from the moment they put up their hand until they become a client.
3. Pricing — and getting it right
4. Selling other services
5. Growing through acquisitions

I said, 'Phil, you are on a journey. It looks simple. It is simple. The important key is that we set a clear path, which we've done with your Strategic Plan Worksheet. Now that we've got the roadmap, my job is to get you to implement your quarterly goals, one step at a time, and to hold you accountable to make sure you do the right things at the right time.

'The sooner we get these changes implemented, the sooner you will be able to make the jump from the SE step fully onto the BO step, and from there onto the I step, as soon as possible,' I said to him.

'Yes, I am really glad I am doing this. It is not that complicated — it is just the implementation of it which has always held me back,' Phil said.

With a smile, I replied, 'Phil, that is exactly why you're working with me. We've got the knowledge, but more importantly, the *process* that will get you to implement the right things at the right time. Our job is to build the machine. To get ten out of ten for each of the corners on the triangle. Because once you've done that, you will make the jump. You will move from the BO step onto the I step. And it will put you into a place where you'll be working the hours and with the clients you choose. Your practice will give you as much money as you desire — meaning that you will have fixed your broken model and you'll be loving every moment of your life.'

For the reader: rate yourself out of 10 for each of the points on the triangle.

If you want a more detailed analysis which will give you an instant snapshot of your practice, you can go onto www.accoa.co.uk/thehighlyprofitableaccountantworksheets where you can download a sheet that will give you the exact rating we give our clients. We use a martial arts belt grading system, and most people who start with us are at a white belt level.

The aim of the game is to put the systems in place and get yourself to black belt.

To see where you are at the moment, download the questionnaire and complete it for yourself.

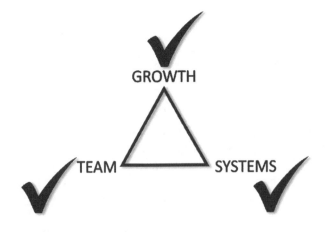

6. TEAM

Phil was getting really excited. For the first time in his life, he could really understand where he was, exactly what the roadblocks were and he was eager to get started.

But at the same time, Phil was exhausted and feeling overwhelmed. He could see the light at the end of the tunnel, but also knew that it was going to be a bit of a hard slog to get there... or put differently, it was going to be a hard slog, whether we did anything or not.

'Might as well make the hard slog count for something,' I joked.

'Rudi, I am working long hours. When things go wrong, I am always the one who has to be there to pick up the pieces. My team is okay, but I can't quite trust them in the way I'd like to be able to trust them. I feel like I'm on a treadmill and it is just hard work. I'm not complaining, because this is what I have to do to feed my family, but heck — I wish there was a better way,' Phil grunted.

In this section, we're going to look at six areas that we covered with Phil in order for him to make some dramatic changes to his team. I'll show you how it all fits together and how it operates in a profitable way.

We're going to take a look at:

1. What exactly is a 'Profitable Practice Model'?
2. Who is the first person that you need to control?
3. What exactly is an A+ team (and do you have one)?
4. How do we recruit the right people?
5. How do we move the wrong people on?
6. Outsourcing — how to make it work.

1. What Exactly Is A 'Profitable Practice Model'?

When I started working with Derek, they were a three-partner firm with about 45 staff. They were profitable but they were all rushed off their feet. The amount of money they had locked up on outstanding debtors and Work-In-Progress would have gone some way towards paying a substantial deposit on a Learjet.

'What exactly is a Profitable Practice Model?' was one of the questions we had to ask ourselves.

Please be aware, as you read further, that I am sharing with you some standard ideas. It is always important that you take these ideas and then find a way to transform them so that they can work for you in your world. At the end of the day, there is no 'one size fits all'. But there are some universal concepts that you can transform into your own way. And it is irrelevant whether you are turning over £70,000 per year or £70 million per year — the universals still stand.

My benchmark for profitability: the range for Net Profit Before Partners Drawings is between 20% – 40%. Less than 20%, we are making some obvious mistakes that should be fairly straightforward to rectify. When we are above 40% we are on the right track. The 50%-ers are doing well. And then there are a few superstars above 60%.

Here are some of the concepts that may be present in our Profitable Practice Model.

The Guard Dog

At the front door we have a Guard Dog.

Our Guard Dog is an admin person who has the personality of a bull dog — strong, fierce, can be gentle, is completely and utterly persistent and will *never* give up. This person stands at the door of our factory. And this person has access to a lot of checklists.

Checklist + Tenacity makes up the Guard Dog's job.

The Guard Dog's job consists of getting *everything* we need from a client *before* we start the job. Which means that once a job goes into our 'factory', there will be *no* hold-ups or delays.

Should anything go into the factory and it is then discovered that actually there was something missing, it immediately gets passed back to the Guard Dog, who then:

1. Updates that client's checklist so that the same error does not get repeated the following year; and
2. Tenaciously and persistently starts chasing the client for this outstanding item(s) until we have it.

On the day the work goes into the factory, the Guard Dog logs that date. Because our Guard Dog is also responsible for recording and reporting for the duration of work inside the factory, our Guard Dog will have access to the date the work is completed — at which point another date is logged. Date 2 less Date 1 is our turnaround time.

The Pods

Inside our factory we have pods. A pod typically consists of three or four people, including a pod manager. Pods are set up in such a way that it is very clear what that pod is responsible for. Depending on your world, it could be a niche or specialism. Or quite frankly, it could be clients' surnames/company names A–G; H–P; and so on. Whatever works for you in distributing the work fairly and equally amongst your pods. But each pod has to know exactly what it is responsible for.

The beauty of pods is that it brings responsibility and therefore accountability. When we track pod KPIs, the pods will in a friendly way start to compete against each other (e.g. Pod 1's turnaround time is 60 days and Pod 2's turnaround time is 45 — I promise you that in one way or another, at some point Pod 1 will start changing things so that their days improve).

Outsourced Team Members

Yes, chances are pretty good that in the competitive world economy that we live in, we could find the same calibre of person as we'd be paying in our home country in another economy where it costs us a quarter or a third for the same skill level. There are a whole host of reasons why this shouldn't work. But at the same time there are a host of excellent reasons why this can, and should, and does work when done correctly. This means that some of our pods or pod members are based in another office... which just happens to be in another country. Nothing wrong with going international — there are very few large or corporate organisation on this planet who haven't in some form or another done this. In order to stay competitive, we have to figure out how to get this one to work.

Our Customer Care Manager

You can give this any title you want, but this is our friendly, happy, fairly extroverted, great communication-ability customer-facing staff member.

This could be you, but ideally these are managers who can connect with your clients. Their job is to ensure that our clients are super happy. That the work is done on time.

Once the work has been logged and gone into the factory, a call from the Customer Care Manager to the client gets made to let the client know where things are and roughly the duration before we expect to get the job completed.

Once work has been completed, it is the Customer Care Manager who meets up with the client to take them through the work completed according to a fairly strict standard agenda.

The Customer Care Manager is the touch point for the client. Their job is to ensure that we end up with raving fans.

You

And then of course we have *you* somewhere in that mix as well. So what exactly is your job? Well, besides setting direction and leading... pretty much anything you want it to be. Ideally you are involved in generating new business, being the face of the company, making speeches at charitable events, going on lots of holidays and generally having a great time. And perhaps working with a few clients of your choice whom you really enjoy.

And fair enough — right now that may not yet be where you are, or even where you see yourself.

But always have this motto in the back of your head: 'My job is to work myself *out* of a job.'

Admin

It is well known that accountants (and partners) spend an inordinate amount of very expensive time on all kinds of low-level admin tasks. That is like saying, 'Andy Murray, please come and help because we need someone to put up the net on the tennis court. Usain Bolt, help because we need someone to paint a white line on the running track. Richard Branson, please help serve some drinks in the plane's cabin.'

With all due respect, I am absolutely certain that if any of those individuals were actually asked to do any of those tasks, they'd be more than happy to oblige. But that isn't the point. The point is that we all have strengths. And weaknesses. And when we play to our strengths — that is when it all works beautifully.

When a £500 per hour partner (or £100 quite frankly), spends time filling in admin forms, or moves around a box of paper, or makes a photocopy, or calls up a client to chase them for X, Y or Z, which could as easily have been done by a £15 per hour person, that is just plain wrong thinking...

It is a vital step towards profitability to list everything that is done by expensive people (who could earn money by doing expensive things) that could just as easily be done by lesser expensive people, even with only a bit of training or some checklists.

It is estimated that an average of two hours per day per accountant is wasted on admin tasks that could as easily have been done by a less expensive admin person.

Here is a list of 25 such tasks that are typically done by accountants that should be done by a much less expensive admin person who has the right training and checklist to follow.

1. Client additions and deletions
2. Returning client records
3. Typing of letters and simple reports to clients
4. Filing
5. Dealing with client correspondence

6. Making and changing appointments
7. Fee preparation
8. Preparing checklists of information required from clients
9. Reviewing and checking client source documents when received against checklists
10. Contacting clients for any missing information or general queries
11. Logging of each job on the Job Register
12. Collation and preparation of electronic workpapers
13. Preparation of the first draft of job budgets
14. Monitoring of WIP
15. Monitoring workflow
16. Advising clients of VAT registration
17. Advising clients of personal income tax assessments
18. Advising clients of tax file number
19. Review and forward clients' running balance account from Inland Revenue
20. Printing and binding finalised annual financial statements, taxation returns, etc.
21. Incorporation of companies
22. Completion of annual company returns
23. Monitoring work checklists to meet Inland Revenue due dates
24. Review and chase debtors at the end of each month
25. Systems writing and updating

Want to have some fun with a simple exercise?

Do this sum for your own practice:

1. # of accounts staff: _____
2. # of hours per day potentially to be handed to an administrator: _____
3. Average charge-out rate: _____
4. Total of the top 3 multiplied by each other: _____
5. Times by 23 working days per month: _____
6. Times by 11 working months: _____
7. **Total:** _____

Scary number, isn't it? That's the number of hours and profits you are wasting.

Finance

Why is it that accountants are the only people who absolutely insist on doing their own company's accounts — no matter whether they're turning over measly amounts or turning over millions?

'Because I can, so I will!!!'

Keep in mind, the aim of the game is to get as much off your own shoulders as quickly as possible. So this is something that you want to let go of as soon as you can.

'But Rudi, I can't trust anyone in my business to do this! I don't want them to see my numbers.'

Well, if you truly have an A+ team, then why not? If you are of big enough size, then hire a full-time person to do this for you. Or get a part-timer to do this for you. Or get an outsourcer to do it for you. All of those alternatives I have seen clients of mine use very successfully.

Bradley is managing partner in a three-partner practice. At our quarterly group meetings he would always have excuses for why he did not have his numbers available. The real reason was that the numbers were created by one of his partners – and accountability and responsibility was an issue. Eventually he made a decision to get a full-time financial controller in place, and suddenly the entire financial function, including credit control, was working.

Melony is turning over only about £300,000 per year. She moved her own accounts onto Xero, went through a process to find a qualified accountant in the Philippines to do her accounts for her and this person's full-time salary works out to about £500 per month.

It was done in different ways, but both Bradley and Melony are now on top of their management accounts.

When someone else is doing it, you can make them responsible to get it to you on a certain date. And you can hold them accountable if it is not done. You can apply a lot of pressure if you need to in order to ensure it gets done properly. When you or a partner is doing it, there are always going to be missed deadlines, because this is not really one of your priorities. Accountability is not as strong. Plus, every minute you are wasting on this admin function is a minute you are not out there generating more business.

Finance — get it *off* your shoulders.

Set a date... and this Friday could not be soon enough!

2. Who Is The First Person You Need To Control?

As a kid, I remember a friend once telling me a story of two tribes.

'Those were terrible years. Lots of bloodshed. The wars started when I was a young boy. A lot of people died. We were living in fear that our homes would be burned.

'There was the story of the generals. One on our side, the other on their side. Each general was leading his own army. Their general, he was well known for being a disciplined man. They called him Shaka Zulu. He was a very demanding warrior. He demanded that his troops practice every day. For hours on end. He would get them to run over thorns with bare feet in order to strengthen their feet... but also their endurance, and their minds. And if he lost impis in practice, he was happy to pay that price as part of the preparation.

'Our general on the other hand was a different type of man. He was a bit of a womaniser. He liked parties. And he drank a lot of beer. Too much practice wasn't particularly his thing. And running over thorns — well, why would anyone want to do that? And besides, the weapons we were carrying we've had for generations.

'Needless to say, we were taken completely by surprise by Shaka's army. They wiped us out. They took our women, and the surviving men and boys were invited to join his army — or die. I chose to live.'

That is how the story goes.

But the moral of that story?

The troops are always a mirror reflection of the leader.

And much more than that...

Right now, when I look around myself in my world, I am seeing a reflection of me.

Everything around me that I see which makes me happy is a reflection of me.

Everything around me that I see which makes me unhappy is also a reflection of me.

Things that work are a reflection of me, and things that do not work are as well.

If I am wealthy with a lot of investments, that is a reflection of me; but if I am highly indebted and about to declare myself bankrupt, *that* is a reflection of me. If I am driving an old worn-out car that I can barely afford the petrol for, that is a reflection of me; if I am driving a Bentley which was paid for in cash, *that* is a reflection of me. If my team around me irritates me because they are unproductive and unprofitable, that is a reflection of me; if my team around me is awesome and they are also super productive and highly profitable — that is a reflection of me.

Everything in my world, at some level or another, is a reflection of me.

If, instead of only me, there are a number of partners who make up the leadership team, then everything around them and within that organisation is a reflection of that leadership team.

As the saying goes 'When I change, it changes'.

If you want to see the changes around you, yes, by all means you are going to make changes to systems and to people. But most importantly (and nothing happens if this does not happen), *you* have to change. You have to change the way you do things. You have to change your mindset and your beliefs about how certain things are, or how they are not. You have to change certain habits and the way you've always done things.

As *you* change, your surroundings will change.

I recall once working with three partners of a firm. And I remember vividly them coming to a number of coaching sessions and saying, 'The biggest challenge we have with our team is that they are always late with their work. And they never do things they say they will do.'

That was an opportunity for me to point out that:

1. The three of them were almost *always* late for their coaching sessions

2. It was very rare that they actually complete all their goals they'd committed to.

And yet, that was the very thing they were complaining about.

With that blatant realisation, the three of them immediately began to change their ways.

And for some unknown reason, their team changed their ways.

The troops are always a mirror reflection of the leader.

So the place where all of this starts?

It starts with you.

The problem with that of course is that we all have our own blind spots. We simply don't see the things we can't see. And this is one of the places where it is absolutely invaluable having a great accountability partner or coach. Because they will gently give you feedback about the things that you are simply, completely and utterly unaware of.

And as this awareness is created and you start changing, guess what starts happening in the mirror reflection around you?

Miracles start happening.

When you try to make the changes to the Team-Systems-Growth triangle whilst ignoring the above point, it will feel like you're swimming upstream and that you're just not getting anywhere.

Your blind spots — the ones that you are completely unaware of — are the biggest arguments for having an accountability partner or a coach on your side.

So what are some of the blind spots that you are going to have to conquer if you truly want to master the BO step and jump to the I step?

There are many of them, but here is a fundamental one:

'I'm too busy, I don't have enough time.'

That sentence is the #1 thing that I hear almost everyone I meet say when we start working together. Which is why we've developed a very robust process to help our clients get more time, which we implement from the first week of working together. This process will last anywhere from four to twelve weeks. Because, if you don't have time, you won't have time to do the things that need doing in order to implement some of the processes we are going to cover in this book.

Here are some key pointers:

Default Diary

You have to take your own time very seriously. You cannot continue being the victim of other people's whims and ways. Your diary cannot stay open for anyone to jump into anywhere whenever they feel like it.

It is your life. Your diary. Your time.

You take control.

You are not running an Accident & Emergency service at your local hospital. In your world, most emergencies can wait a few hours. If you were called to a hospital because your kid had just been hit in a hit-and-run accident and at that point in time, a client wanted to get hold of you... well, quite frankly, in most cases, they're going to have to wait a few hours or even a few days till you can get back to them.

That logic holds for most times when clients want to get hold of you. When you are in a meeting — door shut, your phone switched off. When you choose to be uninterruptable and be totally *there*, focused in the moment, others will respect that you will be available again in a few hours and that you will then see to them or return their calls. Absolutely nothing wrong with that.

Does this require you doing things a little differently than before?

Probably.

Does this require a certain level of self-discipline?

Yes.

Does it require a certain level of self-belief and valuing of your own time?

Yes.

Does it require that you put your life and your priorities into perspective?

Yes.

Is this fundamental to you taking yourself and your organisation up to a next level?

Absolutely!

One of the best ways to make this happen is to develop certain timeslots in your standard/average week which are blocked out for certain activities. And these time blocks do not get moved for *anything*!

Time to meet with your team to review how the past week went and what is planned for the coming week.

Time for a marketing meeting to get an update.

Time for production meetings.

A block of time to work on your business for at least two hours every single week.

A weekly quick debtors' review meeting, a day purely for client-generation meetings, or for internal work and reviews, or perhaps a whole day where you are available for clients or team members for any queries they may have.

I don't want to be prescriptive on what needs to be in your diary. But when you build into your diary specific days for specific activities, and then within those days certain timeslots for certain things — and then you *rigorously* keep to these planned slots... *that* is when your output as a business owner will increase tenfold.

And you will see the results very soon!

If this is a weakness for you, get yourself a PA to run your diary for you. You book absolutely *zero* into your diary. He or she is 100% responsible for *all* bookings into your diary. His or her job is to keep your designated timeslots open and to manage your world. They will be responsible and accountable to make that happen. And if it slips, you hold them accountable.

Email Management

Again — the aim of the game is to let go. Let go of as much as you can and delegate it to others.

You have to find a way that works for you, but let me share with you two examples.

Mark came to me and said, 'Rudi, I get hundreds of emails each day — it takes up a HUGE amount of my time. What can I do about this?'

In Mark's case, he had a team member he could think of whom he could trust to manage his emails for him: his office manager, Sharon. So we set up a new email address for Mark which he only gave out to a very select few people. Sharon then took over his main account, and she would deal with 90% of his emails by either forwarding it onto the right person to deal with it, or responding herself, saying, 'Mark is incredibly busy at the moment, but you are very important to him and he's asked me to deal with your query on his behalf.'

I remember Mark going on a two-week holiday once where he opened no emails, and when he came back, he had about eighteen emails to deal with. Through the changes we brought about, Mark is now only working three days a week in his practice.

A similar scenario: Ben came to me with the same story. He was getting an influx of emails each day and it was taking an inordinate amount of time to get through it. When I asked Ben if there was anyone in the firm he could trust with his emails, his first response was the standard I always seem to get: 'But there are lots of sensitive emails that I wouldn't want my staff to know about — emails from my partners discussing staff and salaries and so on.'

Of course — but... is there anyone in your team that you trust *enough*? If you sat down with them and told them that you were going to put them into a role where you would be placing an enormous amount of trust in them, would they be up for it and rise to the challenge? With of course a penalty of death should anything ever slip out and you find out that they were the source (okay... that is just a joke — we're not *really* penalising so harshly).

The reality is that when you have an A+ team around you, there is normally someone like this. And if not, then you do not actually have an A+ team around you.

So Ben decided that he did have such a lady on his team: Jean. But she was a reception/admin person, so there were loads of emails she would have no idea how to handle. But he did trust her that should she see sensitive emails, she'd be able to treat it as sensitive information.

Great. Next question. 'Who on your team could you trust to deal with non-sensitive emails for you?' After a bit of thinking, Ben decided that Jess was a team leader and she knew enough about the work as well as about the business that she would be able to deal with that.

So it was arranged that going forwards Jean would have access to Ben's inbox. About 10% of the emails she could deal with directly. About 70% of the emails she could pass onto Jess to deal with. And the remaining 20%, that only Ben could deal with, she'd forward onto him.

Ben had to sit with Jess and look at some of the work she was doing. After some thinking, Ben identified a few of her lower-level tasks that could be handed over to another team member which freed up the necessary time in Jess's diary to deal with Ben's bulk of his emails.

We set up a new email address which Ben guarded with his life and only handed out to his partners and a few other very select people.

As a further example of delegating to trustworthy team members that can handle sensitive information, my PA is very trustworthy — and she is based in the Philippines. All my emails get scanned by her first, and only emails that she cannot deal with will end up in my inbox.

My point is, it is not only possible for you to free up time in ways such as this, but in order for you to change things, it is essential.

In order for your *practice* to step up to the next level, it is imperative that *you personally* step up to the next level. This requires a step-up in leadership — yourself first. This can be a hard task when you try and do it by yourself. One of the simplest options to help and guide you here is to get hold of an accountability partner or a coach who can help you with this. It is important that you find the right person for this journey. The person you select to help you with this is going to intimately understand both your strengths and your weaknesses. And their job is to help you stretch further than what you ever thought possible for yourself.

3. What Exactly Is An A+ Team? And Do You Have One?

Phil's favourite complaint seemed to be about how he couldn't really trust his team and the very long hours he ended up working due to this lack of trust.

As a business owner, you are either looking forwards building your business, or you are looking backwards fixing your team and their troubles. Once you've decided on your BHAG in your Strategic Plan, you must treat it as if you are going for the Olympic gold.

And when we are going for the Olympic gold, we need an A+ team behind us.

It is completely okay having a B or a C team behind you. Just do recognise that you are *not* going for the Olympic gold. Accept that fact, and stop whining about how unhappy you are about the long hours you're working. That's the choice you've made.

'But Rudi,' Phil said, 'rather the devil I know than the one I don't know, right? And recruitment is hard! What if I can't find anyone to replace these people? I'd be left with huge gaps and not be able to deliver to my clients!'

'I hear you, Phil. But before we decide that you have a bad team, let's take a few minutes to figure out exactly who you have in your team,' I said to him.

Here is a simple formula to determine who you have in your team. I developed this formula as a very simple way to figure out exactly what you have in your team.

The formula is:

$$A + A = A+$$

First A stands for 'Attitude' (towards life in general). Second A stands for 'Ability' (in your current role).

Rate a person for each of those from zero to ten, with zero being 'useless' and ten being 'superman or woman'. Then get an average of those two numbers.

My rule of thumb is that if someone has less than an eight, we have to ask ourselves why this person is in our team.

'So by way of example, Phil, let's take you. Quick gut-feeling answers, please.'

Phil said, 'Attitude? I guess I'll give myself a nine. Ability? Hmmm... nine.'

'Okay,' I said to Phil, 'that gives us a nine average. Great — glad to have you on our Olympic team!'

And so we very quickly listed every member of Phil's team and scored them.

Here are a few examples of Phil's team members:

	Attitude	+ Ability	= A+ :8
Phil	9	9	9
Jenny	10	10	10
Jack	8	6	7
Joe	4	9	6.5
Lucas	6	5	5.5

There are some rules about the two lefthand A's in our equation.

When it comes to a low score in Attitude:

1. I am not certain that I want to keep on paying you for the next ten years whilst you think about shifting your attitude.
2. The problem with having someone on your team with a low score in Attitude? It only takes one rotten apple in the cart to destroy the entire cart!
3. Sometimes it might be a motivation problem which you might be able to influence.
4. Keeping low Attitudes in your organisation is incredibly risky — and not worth the hassle.

Low scores on Ability tend to be either:

1. The individual is the right person for the business (in other words, their Attitude rating is 8+), but they need some more training to uplift their skills. As the leader in the organisation this responsibility sits squarely on your shoulders.
2. Or alternatively we have a situation of a square peg in a round hole. We have the right person in the organisation, but they are in the wrong role. Purely as an example, let's say that we have a highly analytical accountant type in our organisation who is trying to do telesales. In a million years that is just never, ever going to work. In this case, we have to ask ourselves if we have another role for this individual within the organisation. Because if we don't, then we have to move that person on out of our organisation — which then sets them free to go and find another job where they will be much happier in doing what they are really good at.

Looking at the sample of staff members on Phil's list,

1. Jenny: 10 Attitude, 10 Ability. She is awesome. Keep her, whatever it takes.
2. Jack: 8 Attitude, 6 Ability. Phil realised it was a training issue and went and had a chat with Jack. Between them they came up with a specific list of things that Jack will learn and work with, plus a specific timeframe for completion. A mentor has been allocated to specifically work with Jack as he progresses through his training.
3. Joe: 4 Attitude, 9 Ability. The classical mistake. As seen on his CV, it is someone who clearly can do the work. But personality-wise and Attitude-wise, Joe is actually causing a whole lot of disruption to the team, despite the fact that he is really good at what he is doing. Phil had to make a tough decision. He realised that if he had his heart set on going for the Olympic gold, then he could only tolerate an A+ team behind him. After consulting with his HR consultant, Phil made the decision that Joe was not the right member for his team, and a process was started that took a few months before Joe was moved on out of the team and they could work on finding relevant replacements.

4. Lucas: 6 Attitude, 5 Ability. Phil realised that besides the fact that Lucas was actually dragging the team down, he was more of a square peg in a round hole and it would be best to move Lucas on. Phil again went to the HR consultant to start a process that would see Lucas moved on.

In a conversation I had with Phil, he admitted that it was really tough for him to go through the process of letting both Joe and Lucas go. But he persisted with it — and he did eventually find A+ replacements for his team.

Phil was over the moon with the respect he had gained from his remaining team members as a result of his actions. A number of his team said that they were glad that he did what he did and that he should have done it a long time ago.

Productivity was up. There was a different vibration in the office.

However, because Phil had worked for a number of years with both Joe and Lucas, he found it incredibly hard to do what he did. He had numerous sleepless nights over this issue.

But now that it was done and he was on the other side of it, not only did he feel much better about himself and stronger within himself for facing up and doing what he knew needed doing, but he also felt a sense of freedom and relief.

Knowing that he is in charge of his own destiny.

And that he is the one steering the ship.

Leadership is about doing the right thing. Not the comfortable thing.

4. How Do We Recruit The Right People?

Phil said to me, 'Rudi, I now know who I have in my team, but what do I do about it? Where do I find the right people for my A+ team?'

That is when I explained to Phil that there is a five-step process when it comes to recruiting new people

Step 1: Know the Role
Step 2: Craft Your Ad
Step 3: Cast Your Net
Step 4: Check the Net
Step 5: Reel Them In

Step 1: Know The Role

The very first step that most people miss when it comes to recruitment is the exercise I'm about to describe to you.

Mindmap

We are going to create a mindmap.

Take a blank A4 page and in the centre of it draw a small circle. Inside the circle, write *Our Perfect...* and then fill in whichever role you are recruiting for.

Next, mindmap twenty different words onto that page that describe *only personality* of this perfect person for that role. Therefore, words or concepts such as *Good at IT* or *Ten years' experience* are *not* for this list.

But words such as *Good communicator, Team player* and the like *are* for this list.

No cheating. Keep going till you have twenty words on that page.

After that, the next step is to review that list of twenty words and then highlight the three words that you would consider are the most important for this person in that role. Yes, all twenty words are important. But pick three. These key words will differ for differing roles in your practice.

These central three keywords are vitally important. When you find your ideal person, they must be able to 100% absolutely tick all three of those words. This is non-negotiable. Sometimes we get two *Yes*es and one *Maybe*. Maybe is *not* a yes, so it sits under the *No* umbrella. If you are serious about finding an A+ team, then this is very, very important.

Once you know those three keywords, keep them in mind — you are going to be using them in your job ads and in your job description. They will also be at the forefront of your mind during the selection process, because anyone who has a *No* or a *Maybe* on those three main words does not belong in this role in your organisation.

Roles Chart

We also need to have a written-down roles chart.

This looks a bit like an organisational chart.

You can find templates in Microsoft Word/Insert/SmartArt/Hierarchy to see what this looks like. Or you can simply insert boxes into an excel spreadsheet.

Basically we are going to have three sections.

Start with Managing Partner at the top — we always want a single person in charge (we'll explain further in this book when we cover the Who-What-When triangle why this is so important).

Under this, let's connect the roles (with no names at this stage).

The three sections of the practice:

1. Production (this is everything involved with the delivery of our service)
2. Finance and Admin (this is the glue that holds it all together)
3. Marketing (this is about getting new business in through the door)

Now under each section draw boxes below which represent the roles under each section. Generally, you'll have a manager or managers and underneath them support roles.

Only after you've drawn all the different roles as you have them in your practice do you start putting names into those boxes. You might find on this first draft that some names are repeated in far too many boxes (especially your own).

The step after that is to repeat this exercise, but now draw the boxes in the way you would like the roles to be at some point in the future — perhaps 12 or 24 months forwards.

And again, put names in the boxes where you would like them to be — some of those boxes will have A.Nother in them for roles you need to recruit for.

So far we've figured out exactly the perfect person for our organisation. We are 100% clear on where they (and everyone else) fits into the organisation.

Now it is time to go to the next step, which is...

Step 2: Craft Your Ad

Even if we decide that we are only going to use recruitment consultants, we still need to do this exercise, because by writing it down, it really clarifies what and who we are looking for.

We craft the job ad in 'You' language. When you've completed the ad writing, count the I's and We's, and then count separately the You's. The You's should far outweigh the I's and We's.

At the end of the day this is a sales letter, and good sales copy is always written from the perspective of the person who reads it — and the thing they want to read most about is... themselves.

A job ad that is written in the format of *We are this and we are that and we have been here for 100 years and we, we, we...* versus *You will have fantastic opportunities and you will love your working hours and you will...* The 'You' format is definitely better!

Keep in mind a golden rule about writing your job ad.

Be a little cheeky. We are using *deselection*. In other words, we are pushing the wrong candidates *away!*

Here is a basic format that can be followed.

A fantastic opportunity has arisen at [OUR PRACTICE] for a [ROLE] for someone who is [KEYWORD 1], [KEYWORD 2] and [KEYWORD 3].

You will be responsible for EXCITING THINGS, EXCITING THINGS, EXCITING THINGS.

You will gain BENEFITS, BENEFITS, BENEFITS when you work with us.

If this job ad describes you and what you are looking for, then give us a call.

Once you have written your ad, you will have incredible clarity on exactly who you are looking for — as well as incredible clarity on which candidates you have to say *No* to.

Here is an example of what such an ad might look like.

Accountancy Practice requires Dynamic Manager

Looking for a new challenge?
You have a lot of potential, but currently going nowhere?
Are you ready to grow with us?
Want to be actively involved in taking our Practice to the next level?

Exciting management role at Accountancy Practice in XXXX.

Due to continued growth and development, XXXX is seeking a dynamic person who will be pivotal in helping take your XXX office into the future.

We currently have X staff in X offices in XXXXX, XXXX, XXXX, XXXX and a practice wide agenda for growth. Qualified managers lead each office.

Have a look at our website – XXXXXXX

You will be described as:

Ambitious, a great communicator, a great manager, someone who wants to make a difference to our clients' lives, organized and efficient, a make-it-happen person.

Someone who can take charge of any situation and provide leadership to staff and clients.

Someone who really gets a kick of helping clients and bringing real value to their businesses and their lives.

Someone who wants to make a difference and put their mark on whatever they do.

The job is:

Initially you will be 2nd in charge in XXXXX to the MD, XXXXX but this is only temporary. In the long run, you will take over the running of the XXXXX office and be responsible, with the team, to grow this practice 4x in size over the next 5 years. You will also be a part of building the team to deal with the growing office workload.

You will have all the assistance and training you need, but this role definitely requires a go-getter personality.

A broad background of experience is required including accounts, general tax, charities and audit and a track record of supervising staff and dealing face to face with clients.

Job location:
You will be based at our XXXXX office but we travel all over XXXXX

Salary range:
From XXXX to XXXXXX including incentives

To a large extent you will be your own boss and have a lot of freedom.

This is a challenging role and not for the faint hearted.

If you believe you are the right person for this job, then send me your CV, contact details and a short e-mail explaining why you think that you are right for this job to:

XXXXXXX

Opportunity is calling for the right person.

Step 3: Cast Your Net

Next step is to get your ad out there in a very systematic way. The one place where most people fail here is the lack of persistence and follow-up.

Here are some ideas:

1. Recruitment Agencies
2. Websites
3. Colleges
4. Incentivise Your Staff
5. Facebook
6. LinkedIn
7. Personal Network

1. **Recruitment Agencies**: Follow up on a weekly basis and keep track in a spreadsheet exactly when and who you spoke with.

2. **Websites**: Go into Google and type the role as if you are looking for that job in your area. Whichever website is ranking highest at the moment for that search, that is where you want to place your ad. Some sites are free, some you have to pay. It is okay to invest the money. Once the ads are live, have them checked on a weekly basis to ensure they are still live and coming up in the searches. This is an area where a lot of people fall down when I speak with them. They place an ad and think it is live when it either isn't or something is wrong with the ad itself.

3. **Colleges:** Let local colleges know that you are looking for good people.

4. **Incentivise Your Staff**: If a staff member introduces someone who starts working with you, offer to pay them e.g. £200 once the person has stayed for at least two months.

5. **Facebook**: Ask every one of your staff to post the job opportunities on their personal Facebook pages — you never know who they know.

6. **LinkedIn**: LinkedIn has a recruitment package that is worth trying out. Get in touch with them directly to advise you on your options here.

I don't necessarily recommend that you use the following method, but someone once mentioned it to me, so I'll insert it here so that you may be aware of what others might be doing. Specifically look at other accountants in your area and their staff members. When you see someone who you like the look of, send them a message to the effect of 'Hi [NAME]. Came across your name and thought of you. This message may be completely irrelevant to you, and if it is I do apologise. But just in case you might know of someone who may be interested, we have a great opportunity at our practice which has come up recently. You can find out more about it at this link: [LINK]. If you do know of anyone who may be interested, I'd greatly appreciate if you could let them know. Kind regards. [MY NAME]'

7. **Personal Network**: I know of one partner at a firm who paid someone in his local BNI chapter £5,000 for referring someone who then became a partner at their firm. Like he said — had that referral come through a recruitment agency, the fee would have been *much* higher.

Step 4: Check the Net

Recruitment is a long-term and persistent game. Once you get the message out there, you have to keep track of exactly which activities happen when, and then on a weekly basis you have to go back and speak to people or refresh ads.

Keep the focus — the results will eventually come.

If you are not getting any responses, then tweaks need to be made. Perhaps it is the wording of the ad. Perhaps it is the salary range offered. Perhaps there is something else that needs tweaking.

Stay on top of this — it is utterly important that you get your A+ team behind you.

Once you have that A+ team in place, it will be a big step towards your own freedom.

Step 5: Reel Them In

At some point the candidates will start coming in.

Before you arrange a face-to-face meeting (which is very time consuming both in preparation and execution), arrange a quick twenty-minute phonecall. This call will let you have a bit of an initial chat, but its main purpose is to be a deselection call. If you detect any reason why you think this person will not be a good fit, fish for this in these twenty minutes — if it is *not* a fit, then *deselect* them. They don't go further in the process.

An example of this might be that the candidate lives two hours' drive from your office and from previous experience you have learnt that such candidates do not stay long-term.

If the candidate passes this step, invite them to a one-on-one interview.

A key component for one-on-one interviews which a lot of people ignore: ensure that you have some form of practical or theoretical test incorporated into the interview.

As an example, if they are applying for a bookkeeping role, at the final part of your interview, put them down in front of a computer and give them a specific bookkeeping task with a time limit to complete to test how well they perform. Or perhaps a bank recon. Or perhaps a theoretical test, e.g. 'You're arriving at a client to help them sort out their debtors. Write down the steps you would go through in order to ensure this job is completed satisfactorily.'

Anyone can impress during an interview. But the final question is always, can they actually *do* this work? And you have to test for that.

If they've passed up to this point, they're onto the next phase, which is to spend half a day or a full day or an evening with you and your team members working in the office. This is a very friendly working experience. Often people will let their guard down during this section of the testing and tell you things which may very well affect your decision.

And the final part is to actually make some reference phonecalls. In these, you are especially asking questions to find out how the candidate has evidenced Keywords 1, 2 and 3 from our earlier mindmap.

No recruitment process is *ever* going to be perfect — but in this process you have taken a lot of steps to try and get the right person in through the door.

Remember that the individual is on a severe trial period. If it doesn't work, then call it a day and ask them to move on sooner rather than later.

Your job is to build an A+ team to stand behind you, and if they won't contribute to that A+ grade, do not waste your time.

Phil told me about some of his biggest learnings within this process: 'Rudi, this process has been a huge eye-opener for me. I've always looked at CVs first, then brought the best people in for interviews based on those CVs. I'd ask a few questions and then hope for the best. I've now realised that my first criteria needs to be their personality (the Attitude side of the equation) in order to get the right people onto my team. If I am satisfied that from an Attitude perspective they are right, only then do I ask about Ability and CV. And I need to actually test for Ability. If I subsequently discover that I've made a wrong hire, my job is to take action fast and not let things linger.'

Well said, Phil!

5. How Do We Move the Wrong People On?

As you go through the exercise of making your practice better, an interesting thing will happen. It is a bit like shaking a bird cage. And inside there are birdies. As you keep on shaking, some birdies will stay, some will fly away and some new ones will fly in.

Jack Welsh of General Electric was renowned for having gone into a huge loss-making corporation and in a few years turning the company around.

One of his rules was: Hire slow, fire fast.

He also brought in a rule of firing 10% of the entire workforce every single year... so if you were in the bottom 10% of your team, you would be out. That practice has now ended — but as harsh as it is, there has to be some value in it, because no one wants to be at the bottom.

So how do you fire fast?

Phil had a manager who had been with him in his practice for the past seven years. For many of those years the relationship was great, but for the last number of years, Phil's profitability had been really low. The manager was on £60k salary per year, but Phil felt that not only was he doing a particularly bad job at managing, his productivity was incredibly low.

He knew in his heart of hearts that the right thing was to let this manager go.

But seven years was a long time. What could he do?

Well, he could continue with a B team behind him and suffer from longer working hours as well as low profitability.

Or he could take action.

At the end of the day, leadership is about doing the right thing, not the comfortable thing.

When you have the wrong person on your team, they will never feel fulfilled as a human being. They are simply there clocking hours.

And you will not be fulfilled either.

So your job as the leader is to move this wrong person on.

This results in two benefits. They are free to find another job that is more suited for them where they can be much happier, and you are free to fill that vacuum with the right A+ team members for your practice.

To take action requires two big steps.

1. Make a decision!
2. Have the courage to pull through with it, no matter what.

Until you make a real decision and draw a line in the sand, nothing will happen.

And if you make a decision, but are too scared to pull it off, nothing will happen either.

We all know that getting this wrong can end up costing a huge amount of money, energy and emotional pain.

It is like walking through a landmine area.

So you definitely want to ensure that you have an HR company behind you to guide you through this landmine area. I would recommend you get hold of a smaller HR company where you can speak directly to an individual (possibly the owner of that business) and explain to them what you want to do so that they can guide you step-by-step.

Solicitors' firms could be an option, but sometimes they can be much more expensive.

There are large HR companies that work more as insurance companies, and to some extent their job is to save their own skin by *not* paying out insurances unnecessarily — so their guidance can be too reserved and you end up *not* moving the person on.

You want someone on your side who totally gets where you are coming from and will then guide you step-by-step through the landmines in order to achieve your goal.

The interesting thing was that after Phil made the decision and got hold of an HR professional who could take him through the process of letting his manager go, but before Phil had yet mentioned anything to this manager, the manager approached Phil... and handed in his resignation.

Sometimes it can be as easy as that.

Keep in mind that any staff member who scores less than eight is questionable.

If it is near an eight, take your time... those individuals are okay for now.

If their average is around a four, then you simply cannot tolerate these individuals on your team if you are serious about achieving freedom for yourself (and remember, these individuals also cannot achieve freedom for themselves while on your team).

But as you can see, I'm not suggesting you change your entire team tomorrow. It is a process that needs to flow in its own time, but it is important that it does happen!

6. Outsourcing — How Do We Make It Work?

On one of our weekly catch-up calls, Phil brought up his concerns regarding outsourcing.

'Rudi, I know you say that as part of our "Profitable Practice" we need some form of outsourced back office. But we've tried this in the past — and it didn't work. We ended up doing the work over and it just took longer to redo the work than if we simply did it ourselves in the first place.

'So having burnt my fingers on this one already, I'm just not convinced this is a good route for us.'

This was how I explained to Phil the three big mistakes that I often see when it comes to getting this wrong.

The Three Mistakes To Avoid When You Outsource

Mistake #1: No dedicated middle person

In order for outsourcing to work effectively, we need a single dedicated person of a sufficiently senior decision-making level with authority to be the go-between between the outsourcers (our back office/team in another geography) and our main office.

This cannot be the partner — it cannot be *you*. You are too busy and your attention won't be sufficiently focused on this and over time it is guaranteed to *not* work.

The person we select as the project manager needs sufficient time to be able to focus on this project, and they need sufficient knowledge and authority to make things happen. They also must know when things are going wrong — and ideally what to do about it to get it back on track.

Mistake #2: Not enough time

It is important that you recognise it is going to take somewhere between six to nine months for this to start working effectively. I can't tell you how many times people have tried this for just two or three months and come back saying, 'This isn't working, we're throwing the towel in.'

The outsourcers have to get used to your way. You have to get used to them. And this process of continuous refining takes about six to nine months. Expect that time span and be prepared and patient for it.

However, having said that, please keep in mind the A + A = A+ formula.

A for Attitude — we need a very high number there, from the start.

A for Ability — it is okay to have a low-ish number when we start out on this journey, as long as we are happy that it really is a training issue, and we are satisfied that our outsourcers are actually taking on and implementing the learnings and the knowledge we are sharing with them.

If you score your outsourcer low on Attitude (friendliness, deadlines missed, etc.) make immediate changes. In that case, waste no time.

Mistake #3: Insufficient continuous feedback

When you start working with your outsourcers/back office, there will be lots of things that you are doing or wanting done that they do not understand.

Enter the middle person.

Your middle person's job is to give continuous, assertive feedback until you have it just the way you want it. Go back to puppy training. The puppy doesn't initially know that it is not allowed to do its business in the house. But over time, every time you see it is in need you pick it up, run outside and get it to do its business outside. And soon enough, the puppy gets what you're on about — and we all live happily ever after.

So there is no point in screaming at the puppy and getting upset every time.

It is simply an exercise in persistence and patience.

Repeating the same pattern until the puppy gets it.

The same is true in training a team member/company/outsourcer in your way of thinking and doing. That same kind of persistence and patience needs to be used in training your outsourcers until you are happy that they completely get it, in the way that you want it.

And in order for that to happen, you have to be patient. When a job comes back *not* in the way you want it, it has to go back with feedback *immediately*. They try again. And again. And again. As many times as needed till they get it.

For that to work, they need constant and continuous and immediate feedback.

Phil recognised that he had made mistakes #1 and #3. Having realised where he had gone wrong before, he was prepared to give it another try.

Where To Find Outsourcers?

There are three main ways to find outsourcers.

1. Outsourcing company
2. Offshoring company
3. DIY outsourced person

Outsourcing companies:

The key here is that our outsourcers are based in a geographic area where their economy allows us to pay a much lesser wage, but still find incredible people to do the work for us.

Outsourcing companies can be based in India, the Philippines or many other countries.

The ability to turn the tap on for more work when you need it, or turn the tap off in your quiet season, is very powerful.

There are a fair number of outsourcing companies out there. Do your own research. Speak to a lot of people and get a feel for how things work.

You can find our recommended resources for outsourcing here: www.accoa.co.uk/thehighlyprofitableaccountantworksheets

Offshoring companies:

Here you are still working with staff members in another country, but the staff member is your own employee. You are responsible for training them, sometimes even flying them to your office, or you yourself fly to them for visits.

Let me repeat again — they are your employees in another country.

Offshoring companies tend to do the recruitment for you and arrange interviews via telephone or Skype with video. You make the hiring decision based on their shortlist of candidates. The offshoring company will then provide office space, desk space and a computer to work at. This will be included in their monthly fee as well as the employee's direct salary on top of their fee.

There are a lot of firms that do this, but a great company you might consider contacting for this is in our recommended resources at www.accoa.co.uk/thehighlyprofitableaccountantworksheets

DIY outsourced person:

When you look for someone to work for you directly, typically they will work from their home, which means their wage is much cheaper than the other options. Typically you can find a qualified chartered accountant for around $500 to $600 per month in places like India or the Philippines.

This does not by any means imply that these people are being ripped off. Their cost of living really is much cheaper than ours and as such their incomes are proportionately lower as well.

The Philippines is an interesting country for outsourcing. America has a very big influence on the Philippines, so the spoken English is very good. Culturally it is more Westernised than a lot of other places. And the work ethic is incredibly high.

Websites where you can start your search for these individuals:

www.upwork.com: Here you register for free, post your job, do your interviews, appoint the right person and then pay them through this site. Upwork will take roughly 10% of each financial transaction.

They've recently brought up Upwork Pro whereby you pay them a once-off $500 per placement and they will be in touch with you to find out exactly what you are looking for. With this brief, they will do the hard work and interviewing and refine the list to a shortlist of three candidates for you to interview. This could be a great time saver.

www.onlinejobs.ph: Here you pay roughly $89 for a quarter's access to CVs on their site, and you can also post your jobs on there. Typically you will pay via PayPal with the standard 2.5% fee.

Technology

There is no one-size-fits-all when it comes to the subject of Technology.

You are going to have to figure this out and fine-tune as you go along. How do you scan and get documents to your outsourcers for them to work on? Do you use online platforms like Xero? Do you have dedicated PCs in your office that they can perhaps access as an option? Do you use Skype to communicate freely?

Whatever the challenges — keep in mind that there is *always* a way.

What Will My Clients And My Staff Think About This?

Client concerns:

Most of us overrate our client concerns.

At the end of the day your clients are concerned about whether they can rate you a ten out of ten for looking after them and their world and providing them with what they need. If they are ecstatic with the service they are getting from you, there are going to be very few clients who care where your team is based.

You might need to bring this into your engagement letters, but this should be fairly easy to achieve.

Staff concerns:

Staff will be concerned about changes and how this will affect their job security.

It is important that you keep an open dialogue with your team throughout this process, from before the start all the way through the finish. Because ultimately we are taking lower level work off their shoulders and they'll be doing higher level work which will add much more value to your clients.

Security:

In my experience, whether you have a crook working for you in your office or on the other side of the planet, it is the same thing. Is it a possibility that either of those scenarios could happen?

Of course it is.

As an employer you do everything in your power to ensure that you have great systems and that your recruitment processes are such that you are able to hire A+ people. But these things happen.

For some of our outsourcing countries, outsourcing forms a significant part of their income, so there are a lot of laws and rules regarding security. Often security in such companies and such countries is higher than in your own office.

Phil was excited. He realised that when he tried it before, he made almost every mistake in the book. And with his newfound perception, he set off to try outsourcing properly this time.

Allow me to share with you where Phil's journey took him after he started implementing some of the items we've covered in this chapter.

1. Phil ended up moving a few of his staff members on because they were simply not a good fit for his team. It was tough, but he did it.
2. He systematically followed the recruitment process and he did in fact manage to find exactly the right people for his team.
3. He actively pushed for outsourcing to work.
4. He found himself a virtual PA who had qualified as a chartered accountant in the Philippines, who is now not only managing his emails and diary, but remotely delegating work.
5. He has delegated his practice bookkeeping and invoicing to that same PA in the Philippines.
6. He changed his team around so that they had much more of a Profitable Practice Model in place with pods.

7. He reduced his own meeting times with clients and is now only personally meeting mostly with A+ clients. His managers deal with the rest.
8. As a person, Phil is constantly growing and developing himself — because, as he now constantly says, 'If I don't change, it doesn't change.'

Those are just a few of the changes that Phil has made to his practice, but it has resulted in him getting much closer to an A+ team. Outsourcing is helping him become even more profitable.

7. MANAGING YOUR DYNAMIC TEAM

I was very proud of Phil and all the progress he had already made!

It was during one of our regular coaching sessions that Phil said to me, 'Rudi, I'm not free yet! How do I manage my team and delegate effectively? I often feel that it isn't quite working. The communications isn't really working as well as it should. Everyone is very busy, all of the time, but the output doesn't really add up if we look at how many hours everyone seems to be putting in. And at the end of the day, I am the one who always ends up picking up all the pieces and doing work in the evenings and coming in over weekends. My wife really isn't happy with this and it all feels a little bit out of control.'

So I asked Phil what he wanted instead.

After a while of silence as he processed my question, he said, 'I want an office where there is a real buzz. An office where everyone is really clear on what they're doing — and getting on with it. And an office where things are just *working*. So that I can end up feeling completely in control. And get my time back again.'

Here are five concepts I shared with Phil. As he implemented these concepts, it completely turned things around and he became really great at managing his team effectively in order to both free himself up and turn his team from an over-reliant team into a fully self-reliant team.

1. The Who-What-When Triangle — The Ultimate Delegation Tool

The tool I'm about to share with you has the power to completely transform your life.

Below you can see the image of a triangle with a *Who*, a *What* and a *When* on each corner.

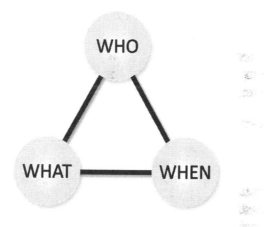

It works a little like a musical triangle. Your job is to get a *ding!* on the triangle. But you can only get a *ding!* when you have a tick next to each of those three corners.

If you haven't got a tick next to each corner, then no *ding!* for you.

Let me illustrate how this triangle works.

Let's say that I work for you in credit control in your practice.

Scenario 1

I come to you and I say, 'I spoke with the lady at the client's office and she said she'll get us paid.'

In that scenario, when I review my Who-What-When triangle, how many corners did we tick?

The answer is one.

We did not have a name for the *Who*-corner and we did not have a date for the *When*-corner. We did have a *What*.

Scenario 2

I come to you and I say, 'I spoke with Mary at the client's office and she said she'll get us paid.'

In this case, how many corners can we tick on the Who-What-When triangle?

Mary is the *Who.* Paying is the *What.*

No *When.*

So only two corners ticked... no *ding!* yet.

Scenario 3

I come to you and I say, 'I spoke with Mary at the client's office and she said she'll get our outstanding money paid. I should have the cheque on my desk by this Friday morning.'

In this case, how many corners can we tick on the Who-What-When triangle?

Mary is the *Who.*

Paying is the *What.*

Friday morning is the *When.*

Finally — a *ding!* on our musical triangle.

Job well done! We've completed our Who-What-When triangle.

But let's take it a step further.

Friday afternoon I either have a cheque in my hand and it gets banked, or there is no cheque in my hand, in which case, without any aggression, I call up Mary again.

I have now closed the one triangle, and I *immediately* open a new one.

'Hi Mary, how are you doing? Mary, last time we spoke you said you'd get the cheque to me by Friday morning. It isn't here yet, what is the next step?'

Mary says, 'Ah, Rudi, I am so sorry. Really, I apologise — our MD who signs the cheques was out on Friday, but he is in this afternoon and I'll get this sorted for you.'

I say, 'Mary, thanks so much, you are great. By when can I expect this cheque on my desk?'

Mary says, 'Definitely by Wednesday.'

'Thanks a lot, Mary.'

We've just created a new triangle and earned another *ding!* There is a single *Who*, a single *What* and a clear *When*.

The reality is that in the world we live in, it is very rare that people will go *beyond* a third triangle. The key is to close one triangle and open another as soon as possible.

Because what is at stake here is not so much the fact that you didn't do what you said you're going to do, but more the fact that we both know that you broke an agreement or a promise.

Breaking one promise... well, anyone could do that. Breaking two promises in a row is pushing it a bit. When you've broken three promises in a row, then this starts raising a different question. What exactly does that say about your character?

We exert incredible emotional pressure by using this method. And the results happen very quickly.

If someone goes beyond a third triangle, then alarm bells should be sounding very loudly in the back of your head.

In every case where you delegate something, it is *up to you* to ensure that you have ticked *every* corner of the Who-What-When triangle.

Which corner do you think people miss out the most on?

Typically the *When* corner, in my experience. Why?

Because if we don't pin someone down to a *When*, it is almost guaranteed to start drifting into Neverland.

Another error I often see is that the *Who* corner does not have a single name, but rather *They, Someone, Everybody* or *John and Jack*.

All of those iterations are incorrect.

We only want a single *Who*. A single name responsible for that project. If John and Jack are equal and both responsible, then pick one of them to be the ultimate responsible person on that project. Flip a coin if you have to.

Only one name allowed.

If you were to list all the things right now that are driving you mad with your team and people you've delegated work to, then go back to the triangle and ask yourself which corner is missing.

Then go back to every one of those people to have a short chat, and ensure that you complete the triangle.

For example: 'John, I know we had a chat about this audit file before and I know you're working on it. Tell me, by when do you think you can get this onto my desk?' In that way, you can close your triangles.

It is your job to record the Who-What-When triangles when you delegate work. It is your job to hold people accountable for *When* they said they'd be ready.

A question I always get is, 'But Rudi, how do I record all of that?'

There are numerous possibilities. Find one that works for you. It could range from a small pocket book to an excel spreadsheet.

One example from a client of mine: she used an excel spreadsheet with columns for *Who, What* and *When*. The *When* had two columns — one for the date she asked someone to do something and the other for the due date. Initially she recorded only three Who-What-When's per day, but very soon she came to realise how powerful this tool was, and she then became much more motivated to use it for all her delegation tasks.

It is your job to follow up for the sake of accountability. Because if you don't follow up, it won't happen and you will suffer the consequences.

And likewise, when you start using this form of accountability with your team, you will find that they will also start thinking in this way. Accountability will vastly improve across the board, and long-outstanding jobs will suddenly be something of the past.

You choose to use the Who-What-When triangle.

Or you choose to ignore it.

Either way, you will get results.

2. Octopus Project Management

Imagine an octopus. It has the body in the middle and then all its tentacles around it.

Your title has just changed.

Your job from now on going forwards is "The Ultimate Project Manager."

Everything that is happening in your world is a project. So you are sitting in the body of the Octopus. Each tentacle is a project. And within each tentacle, within each project, there needs to be a single project manager responsible — who ideally is *not* you.

That way you have someone else within your world who is responsible for a project and they are accountable to you for it and to get it completed.

5-Minute Planning

Here are some very simple but crucial steps for the start of *every* successful project, however big or small.

At the start of each project, sit down with your project manager and:

1. Get your project manager to tell you what the five to ten main subheadings are that they think need to happen to complete the project; write those subheadings down because they become Milestones;
2. For each subheading, decide a due date;
3. The project manager on this project is the main *Who*, but possibly for each subheading, there may be different *Who*'s.

This is a very quick initial brainstorming exercise. It is intended to last less than five minutes.

It allows your project manager in their mind's eye to jot down a quick overview for the project with guideline deadline dates. You can then review this with your project manager and fill in any obvious gaps, or remove any excess steps.

With further research, your project manager may come back with more or less steps, but the idea is that within five minutes you have an initial plan down on paper.

When a new VA joined my business, a task I set her was to find us a new video editor. After a couple of weeks I asked her how she was getting on because the feedback I was receiving from her on this task was minimal.

She hadn't yet located anyone worthwhile.

When I asked her where she had been looking, she told me that she had asked colleagues from her previous work, some friends, a local college and she also tried the website where I had found her. The huge gap that was very obviously missing to me was that she had not yet placed an ad on www.upwork.com, where there are millions of contractors looking for work.

Had I asked her on Day 1, as per the Octopus Project Management concept, what her approach was going to be in five to ten steps, it would have been clear to me from the start, in less than five minutes, that she was missing an obvious idea. Which could have shaved at least two weeks off the time I was now waiting to get a new video editor on board.

Some examples:

Project: Formalise the new partner's partnership agreement.

Who is responsible for this project? John.

What are the main subheadings to bring this to completion?

1. Draw up the agreement
2. Have the legals checked
3. Review
4. Agree and sign

When?

1. 30 July
2. 16 August
3. 25 August
4. 7 September

Project: Introduce Xero into our practice.

Who is responsible for this project? Helen.

What are the main subheadings to bring this to completion?

1. Contact Xero to find out the *What*'s and *How*'s
2. List all the steps that need to happen in order to implement Xero
3. Decide who will be responsible for subsections of this project and allocate responsibilities with dates
4. Do a test with small sample of clients
5. When happy, roll out

When?

1. 26 July
2. 26 July
3. 28 July
4. 17 August
5. 17 September

You can see from the above that these are quick and simple brainstorming exercises. In Example 2, Helen has no idea yet what exactly the steps will be for point #3, but in the overarching, 'Let's sit down and in 5 minutes jot down what the sections are that need covering,' #3 is a main point.

As you can see, the above is not intended to be a definite project plan as such. It is intended to be used as a tool which helps you and your project manager in a matter of minutes to gain clarity on the main direction to be taken to accomplish a specific project.

It is more a guideline to start movement with some deadlines built into it. As we go along the project and we learn more through our research, we can always update steps and dates.

But this is as great a starting point for any project.

1. Make a list of everything that is on your shoulders and weighing you down.
2. From that list, decide what you can transform into the tentacles of the Octopus, what can be transformed into projects.
3. Ensure you create for every project a Who-What-When triangle with high-level subheadings on the *What*'s and a *When* for each *What*.
4. Get yourself out of the tentacles and remain in the body of the Octopus.

And before you know it, you will be able to let go of a huge amount of things that you have never gotten around to that have taken up space in your brain.

Hilene has three partners in her practice with around 50 staff. High WIP days have always been a problem for her, with there being a total of around 7,000 open jobs on the system. Once Hilene learned how to effectively be 'The Ultimate Project Manager' and use the Who-What-When triangle, she created a spreadsheet with those headings of *Who*, *What* and *When* on it.

She then went and sat down with each of her managers. In order to reduce the open WIP jobs, they agreed very clearly what each manager would be responsible for and they agreed on very clear dates.

In her spreadsheet, Hilene listed *every* delegation she made. That way she was able to go back to people where the *When* dates had passed and hold them accountable, creating a new Who-What-When triangle immediately.

Within a period of two months, her WIP was back in control — the first time in *years*!

And that efficiency translated very quickly to extra cash in the bank, which made Hilene and her partners very happy!

3. Passing Back the Monkey

Another frustration of Phil's: 'Rudi, some of my people just don't seem to think for themselves. They keep on asking me how to do things. I wish they could just figure it out for themselves. But if I let them figure it out, that takes ages, and it is so much quicker just giving them the answer or doing it myself.'

I reminded Phil that in order for him to make the jump to the BO step, he needs a self-reliant team. And when he has a dependent team, it is important to keep in mind that often one of the big reasons he still has a dependent team is that he's been the culprit in helping them develop bad habits.

So to change someone from being a highly dependent 'I can't do this unless someone shows me how to do it...' to an independent 'I can figure this out myself', you are going to have to go through another patient and persistent puppy training exercise.

So what do we know about the puppy training phase?

It is a bit messy.

It takes a while.

You have to be very patient and very persistent.

And soon enough, puppy training does come to an end.

From there on, you will probably never need to pick the puppy up and run outside with it to do its business outside again.

Never, ever, ever again.

So that investment of patience and persistence does pay off relatively quickly.

A staff member comes to you and says, 'Phil, I don't know how to do X.'

Your common response might be, 'The answer is Y' or 'To find the answer go and speak to Z'. But when you are in a puppy training phase, both those answers would be incorrect.

Incorrect because if you do respond in one of those ways, then the training you are giving this person is 'Come and ask me because I have all the answers — in fact, if I don't have the answer, come and ask me because I will tell you where to go. That way you don't have to think because I can do the thinking for you.'

So what we're really saying to our team is:

Look at how very important I am.

I am absolutely indispensable.

I am the boss.

I am the best.

I deserve a medal.

'But Rudi — that is a bit harsh, isn't it?' Phil asked.

And I said, 'Yes... it may be.

'But Phil, do you want an overly reliant team, or a self-reliant Team?

'Because if you want a self-reliant team, then you have to take them through a patient process to teach them how to think for themselves.'

And that is the process of 'passing back the monkey'.

So how do we pass back the monkey?

The way to do that is to:

1. Agree
2. Pass it back

When a staff member comes to you and says, 'Phil, I don't know how to do X,' your response might be:

1. *That is a great question!*
2. *What three ideas have you got on how we might do that?*

Depending on the situation, you might sit there with them whilst they explain to you, or you could ask them to go away and come up with some options and return to you at a later stage.

Remember, this is a puppy training phase — it won't last very long, but it does require that you give them the space to think.

And even if the options they come up with are 100% incorrect, that is fine. You are providing the opportunity for them to experience what it feels like to give it a go by themselves. Because before long, they'll figure out how to find the right answers more and more.

A big key is that you keep quiet a lot whilst they come up with the answers. The minute you jump in and 'save' them is the minute where you've just robbed them of a learning experience. Even though the answer is glaringly obvious to you and it is absolutely *jumping* out at you from the page, keep your mouth shut and allow them the space to think, to learn and to grow.

Because on the other side of this process sits your freedom.

Stop 'saving' your team and robbing them from the opportunity to think, to learn and to grow. Allow them to make some initial mistakes in their thinking — it is only through that process that they will learn how to become independent thinkers.

And once their new training has taken hold, then you will find that the only time they will bother you is for much higher level stuff where they genuinely require your input.

Through this process you will move your people much more towards becoming a self-reliant team.

4. The Person Who Says It Owns It

One of the fundamental rules is that 'the person who says it, owns it'.

The person who *creates* it, *owns* it.

Which is one of the reasons that when it comes to delegation, you can decide the *Who*. The *What* is created by that person when they come up with a short list of the main subheadings for a project — *not* you. Because you want *them* to own it, not you. It is *their* project. If they come up with the wrong *What's*, then definitely guide them to the correct ones. But it is vital that the *What* comes out of their mouth! *Not* yours.

Because 'the person who says it, owns it'.

And the *When* — they decide that as well. If you are in disagreement with the *When*, you might respond as follows using the Agree + Ask formula

Let's say that there is a project which John is responsible for and you really want it completed within one month from now, but John responds that he can get it done two months from now.

How do you react to that?

You put your coach's hat on and you guide John to the answer you really want.

'So John, you reckon we could get this done two months from now. Okay, that sounds like a plan *(notice the agreement here: "Yes, I agree it is a plan," not "Yes, I agree with the plan"... subtle but important difference!)*. But I'm thinking we might need it a bit earlier than that. What do you think are some other options to get it done earlier?'

'Well, I guess if we do X, Y and Z differently, we could probably shave off about two weeks.'

'Okay, fantastic. I'm wondering what might need to happen in order for us to shave off even a further two weeks?'

'Hmmm... tough one. But I guess if we add Vicky to the team and work on one weekend, we could probably make it happen.'

'Okay — so John, you reckon that if we do X, Y and Z differently and if we get Vicky in the team and maybe, hopefully not, but maybe work on one weekend, we could get this done within one month?'

'Yes.'

'So that means that if we start tomorrow, we could complete by *[INSERT EXACT DATE 1 MONTH AWAY]*?

'John, you are a superstar! That would be fantastic. Thanks very much.'

Notice how John did all the decision making — he was guided, but the words came out of his mouth, both on the *What* as well as the *When*.

By doing this, you have succeeded in getting your team member to say what he's doing and when. This team member now owns what has been said. And ultimately that means that you can create a fair amount of pressure holding him accountable to this agreement or promise which he's made.

If all of that plan had come out of your mouth, you would possibly have ended up with a disgruntled John, silently cursing you and being completely non-committed and non-caring towards this project.

Always remember that the person who says it, the person who creates it, *owns* it!

5. The Heartbeat

It came as quite a shock when our neighbours announced that they were getting divorced. It was hard on their kids.

It took us a while to get our heads around it as well. They both worked in good jobs. There were no financial difficulties. No extramarital affairs or anything like that. It just ended.

She told my wife that they had stopped talking about things that really mattered. And over time, the break got bigger, until they were essentially two strangers living in the same house. The decision they came to was that it was best for them to go their own ways.

This is a morbid analogy to use for the workplace, but I would argue that this pretty much describes the fallacy of the open plan office.

But we're all in this big open office and we're talking all the time.

Indeed.

But are we talking about the right things?

A good communication rhythm does to a team what a heartbeat does to a body.

A body that is in a coma only needs a very slow heartbeat.

A body that is sitting at a desk needs a slightly faster heartbeat.

A body that is running needs a very fast heartbeat.

An organisation that is in a coma needs a very slow, or no, communication rhythm.

An organisation where only little is happening needs a slow communication rhythm.

And an organisation where a lot is happening and a lot is changing needs a fast communication rhythm.

'But we do have meetings. In fact — we have *death* by meeting! We have meetings every week that go on forever, and they are just wasting everyone's time. It is better not to have meetings!'

I fully agree. Those kinds of meetings are wrong.

So here is a suggested communication rhythm.

1. Daily
2. Weekly
3. Monthly
4. Quarterly
5. Annually

Each of these meetings have a very specific agenda. By keeping to those agendas, you will find that your team knows where it's at, people start getting onto the same page, smoke-screens disappear, productivity increases dramatically and morale goes up. And you will know exactly what is going on in your organisation.

Here is an example of how to set up an agenda for a daily-meeting rhythm.

Daily Meetings

These are typically stand-up meetings where each person has just one minute to talk. Ideally it happens at exactly the same time every day. This meeting is *not* about finding solutions. Solutions are to be discussed *after* the meeting. The agenda for the meeting itself consists of three items.

1. What were you working on yesterday? Your KPIs from yesterday?
2. What are you working on today?
3. What are your bottlenecks?

A response might be:

Yesterday I worked on Clients A, B and C.

Today I'm completing Client A and B and starting on D.

Bottlenecks — the printer isn't working.

What starts to happen in this meeting is that accountability becomes very powerful. Because I said yesterday what I'll be working on, I don't want to keep on getting up day after day repeating the same thing.

Also, it invites solutions to my problems. If the printer has been my bottleneck for the last five days, at some point I'm going to get embarrassed about this same bottleneck and actually do something to get it sorted. Or someone else will hear about my bottleneck and suggest I come and see them after the meeting as they have a solution for it.

This kind of meeting is incredibly powerful. Large corporates around the world use this format with people dialling into a conference call to attend the meeting at a certain time — even from different time zones.

The method mentioned above is one standard way.

But what if people are away from the office on a job? Well, it depends on what rules you put in place to make this happen in your organisation. Do they join a conference call at a certain time to be part of the group? Do they complete a questionnaire and email it through to a central liaison person/office manager on a daily basis who can review it?

There are always ways and means to make this happen.

And when you do make it happen, it will get communication flowing in a way it has never done before in your organisation.

This kind of gentle peer pressure is very powerful.

In the same way, develop specific meeting agendas for a weekly, monthly, quarterly and an annual rhythm.

To download some sample agendas, go to
www.accoa.co.uk/thehighlyprofitableaccountantworksheets

The Summary

Phil was a quick learner. And an even faster implementer.

He went away and printed out an image of a triangle with the words *Who*, *What* and *When* on it. He stuck this onto his wall and started using it immediately. He also explained this triangle to his team so they not only understood what he was doing, but they could also start using this triangle for themselves.

This triangle helped Phil to become more assertive without becoming aggressive. Both him and his team became much more responsible and accountable. Things now rarely slipped past agreed deadlines. They were spurring each other on, using teamwork to promote self improvement.

Octopus Project Management gave Phil a way to let go of control, but he still maintained ultimate responsibility and he was being kept completely in the loop. The result of this was that he was able to delegate more and know that he had a very good method of knowing what was going on.

Passing back the monkeys — this simple strategy very quickly allowed Phil to puppy-train his team to *always* arrive with solutions themselves, even if the solutions were wrong. And because his team started thinking more effectively, over time Phil could see the growth in his team members which allowed him to trust them more and more and allow them greater responsibilities.

The person who says it owns it — again, a great tool for getting his team members to take responsibility. This was a little tough on Phil initially, as he had to get used to a different way. Instead of jumping in and trying to save them, he had to become more patient. But this patience definitely paid off in that responsibility kept on growing within his team.

Team Meeting Rhythm — the strict agendas that Phil now had in place for meetings on a daily, weekly, quarterly and annual basis meant that the team covered all the essential elements of the practice in super quick time. Bottlenecks were quickly identified and dealt with. Which meant that the whole team — and in turn the whole practice — was working like a well-oiled machine.

And the greatest benefit?

This is what Phil told me.

'Rudi... I trust my team now more than ever. Things are just *working*. I am actually able to let go, knowing it will be taken care of. I have been able to get back more time for myself and my family. I get to spend more time at home with my kids. And at work, I now have more time to follow up and push on sales activities. Having an A+ team behind me that is well managed has quite literally changed my world.'

And these were some of the fundamentals that Phil implemented in order to get the tick next to *Team* on the Team-Systems-Growth Triangle.

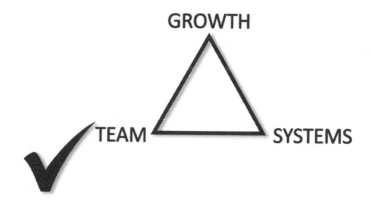

8. SYSTEMS

In the UK, one of the systems that we have is that people drive on the left-hand side of the road.

It is a simple system, but when that system is not followed, it results in car accidents — and even death.

Having systems — and then following those systems — makes the whole thing work.

The other big element which will lead you to freedom is having great systems underpinning the activities of your A+ team.

In the following section, we are going to take a look at some essential systems that you need to have in place to not only support your A+ team, but lead to much better relationships with your clients, improved cash flow, higher productivity... and so much more.

1. The Client Experience
2. Lock-Up and Cash Flow
3. KPIs
4. Becoming Efficient Through Technology

1. The Client Experience

I picked up Phil's message at about 10am and called him back as soon as I could.

He sounded shaken.

He then told me that he had just lost one of his better clients. £18,000 fee gone, just like that, and the client went to KPMG.

Phil had tried to meet up with the client, but the client just wouldn't have it.

Apparently, this client had a bad experience with information coming through to him from one of the managers over the last few months. And yet, Phil's firm had saved this client over £50,000 just in the last year alone.

So what went wrong?

I arranged to meet up with Phil over a cup of coffee. After doing a bit of small talk and catching up, we got onto the subject.

Phil said, 'Rudi... this one really gets me. We're working so hard, yet it feels like we're just standing still. One step forwards and then three steps back. I could scream — this is so frustrating!

'When this kind of thing happens, it tells me that our client retention isn't anywhere near as good as it ought to be. And I'm sure that our word-of-mouth referrals also suffer. I can see it when I look at my practice — even though we are very busy, things are really a bit stagnant.'

'Phil,' I said, 'I totally get how you are feeling at the moment. But help me understand — what is it that you want instead?'

After a few moments of silence, he said, 'What I want instead? I want for our client retention to be as high as we can humanly get it. I want our word-of-mouth referrals to be at an all-time, record-breaking high. What I really want is for our clients to be buzzing with excitement.'

'Okay, Phil. So let's get into this topic. First, let me say this:

'Not only do I totally believe that this is the easiest of all our business growth topics to crack, but it will also provide us with the easy wins.'

Phil gave me a cynical glance. 'Ah, Rudi... if it was all just that easy...' he grumbled with a smile.

So there's a few things that we need to cover here.

Firstly — if you want to stop an attack from the big boys (or, quite frankly, any of your competitors), this is the one place where you can get the upper hand.

If you ignore this part of your practice, they will win.

But if you pay attention to this part of your practice, *you* win.

It really is as simple as that.

'So Phil,' I told him with a smile on my face, 'with that in mind, would you say that it might be worth paying a bit of attention right now?'

He just smiled back, all ears.

First thing to remember... anything in life can be rated from zero to ten, with zero being really bad and ten being really good.

For example: how excited am I about being in the office today? Hmmm... 4. How well did I eat this morning? Well, that chocolate I had on the way here... probably about 6. How happy am I today? 8.

We can rate anything in life.

When you get a new client, you are both in the honeymoon phase, so the relationship is usually a ten out of ten. But then over time, left to its own devices, gravity sets in and that relationship number starts dropping downwards.

Relational vs. Transactional

In what we do as accountants, there are two types of connections we make with our clients.

Transactional Connections and Relational Connections.

A Transactional Connection is when I call you up and we discuss your accounts. Or I call you up and I have a query about your tax. Or you come and see me at the end of the year and we review your finances. Those are all Transactional Connections. This is related to what we do for a living.

When it comes to building, maintaining or improving a relationship, Transactional Connections add very little value and very little bonding to our relationship.

On the other hand, we have Relational Connections. These have almost nothing to do with the work that we do. They are fundamentally different from Transactional Connections. These happen when we meet up for lunch. When you come to my birthday bash. When we go to the cricket grounds together. These are purely social and relational. Relational Connections add massive value and massive bonding to our relationship, which actually improves our Transactional Connection as well.

So we start out with a honeymoon relationship that is ten out of ten on day one.

Over the next three years we certainly have Transactional Connections, but sometimes very limited Relational Connections.

Gravity will automatically set in, and from the client's perspective, that 'ten out of ten' will start dropping down —

Nine...

Eight...

Seven... six... five...

...and even less, if you let it.

Over time it gets comfortable, but it also gets a bit dull and boring.

And then we have our KPMG (or whichever competitor) coming into the marketplace, and I guess what starts happening is a bit like having an affair.

You see, those competitors come in with a 'zero out of ten' relationship to start with. But then something happens. There is an excitement. A buzz. A newness. It is fresh and sparkling. They had such a good seminar. Or the email they sent with the latest news is so very interesting.

And very quickly they are able to push their zero towards a three, and then a five… and with a last-ditch attempt they somehow manage to push their new, exciting, full-of-promises relationship to a six out of ten.

The problem we are faced with at that point in time?

In the client's eyes you are a five and your competitors are a six.

And the universe starts wobbling a bit.

And guess what your next client conversation is going to be like?

'Phil, my wife has a brother. And the brother has an accountant. And this guy is really cheap. And I don't want to do this, but…'

Or any one of 101 versions of that story.

Phil was frowning as I described this concept. 'Rudi, I hadn't quite seen it like that before, but I guess what you are saying does make sense. We had been very focused on the Transactional Connections, because I thought that was what it was all about. But I can see where I went wrong.

'Okay, so how do we fix this?' he asked me.

Let's just make sure we are clear on one thing first:

Relational Connections are all the touches that happen outside of Transactional Connections that cause your clients to sit up and say, 'Wow — these people are really different. I'm impressed. This is great!'

Or think of it this way:

Transactional Connections are what we do.

Relational Connections are what we do to get them to that 'Wow!'

If Transactional Connections are done wrong, and we have a low Relational-Connections number, that is when we lose clients.

When Relational Connections are high, and Transactional Connections still happen, clients will be much more forgiving and will continue staying with us.

Therefore, Relational Connections are the glue that hold it all together.

The good news is that there are two very simple systems that will make you almost 100% immune to attack from most of your competitors, especially the big ones.

We accept and assume that the Transactional Connections happen — after all, if they did not, your clients would be super unhappy! It is the Relational Connections that we need to focus on and ensure that they are definitely in place.

The following two systems, if we don't have them in place yet, need to be implemented immediately. If we have them in place, then we need to fine-tune them to ensure they work perfectly.

Which brings us to the first system:

New Client Onboarding System

The concept of 'onboarding' refers to our process when a new client joins us — all the things we do with them to make them feel right at home and certain that they have indeed arrived at the right place.

One of the big problems with most new client onboarding is that it is heavily weighted to Transactional Connections. There is a lot of form filling and photocopies. Transactions, transactions and more transactions. And then sometimes we are a bit disorganised in what we are looking for and our follow-up is not particularly great.

Which means that not only are we just focused on Transactional Connections, but it also happens very ad hoc.

Sure, our new client is in the honeymoon phase, and we all know how blind being in love can make all of us. When we are newly married, we don't notice any of the little irritating behaviours that we notice in our partners a year down the line. Because in the honeymoon phase we are totally blinded by love.

The problem? We are wasting a massive opportunity. If we focus on implementing a systematic, step-by-step Relational Connection–focused system during the onboarding, not only will our clients be 'blinded by their honeymoon love', but they will be over-the-moon impressed, which will lead to more word-of-mouth, which in turn leads to more referrals and also higher or more fees.

Why would we choose to waste such an opportunity?

'Well,' I hear you say, 'Rudi… I'm just so busy on Transactional Connections–type stuff, I don't have time to think about this "relational" nonsense…'

Sorry to be the bearer of bad news, but this is 100% vital. So how do we get this right?

The simplest way is to sit down with your team, or some of your team members. Draw a 90-day timeline. And brainstorm some ideas on things that could happen within the first 90 days with every new client to impress them.

You want to ensure that this timeline, on the one side, has Transactional Connections. You want to systemise how and when these touches happen so that we completely remove 'ad hoc' from the equation.

But then, on the other side, we also want to timeline our Relational Connections. And this is completely open to your creativity. You and your team can go wild with your ideas here.

First step is to brainstorm ideas. No editing allowed (yet). What could you do that could improve the Relational Connections to really 'Wow!' new clients?

Some possible crazy ideas:

Begin Week 2 with a 'Welcome on board, we're really glad you've joined us!' card… send them a cake, tickets to a football match, tickets to the cinema or perhaps flowers to their office!

Perhaps, during the first four weeks, put in a Relational Connections call once every week.

Week 5, go for a Relational Connections lunch with your new client (or, depending on their client grade, send one of your team members). Ask about them and listen. This serves a dual purpose. On the one hand, it strengthens the relationship even more, and on the other hand, they will tell you their pains — listen for those! This could easily turn into a cross- or up-selling opportunity, or a great opportunity for them to give you referrals.

Week 7, put in another Relational Connections call.

Week 9, send a 'client survey' letter, asking for referrals at the same time.

Week 11, put in another Relational Connections call.

What and how your system looks like is completely up to you and your team's creativity. But do ensure that 1) it gets systemised, and 2) you have a single person (our *Who* on the Who-What-When triangle) who is responsible for ensuring this system is followed.

When you put this in place, you will have systemised your Relational Connections in the first 90 days of a new client joining you.

Do you think that this system might impress this new client?

Do you think it may lead to more word-of-mouth referrals?

Do you think it may lead to more cross-selling opportunities?

I asked these very questions of Phil. With a big smile on his face, Phil looked at me and said, 'Rudi, I can't believe I've not gotten around to this before, but the answer has to be yes, yes and *yes*.'

Customer Service System

The next step is to create a customer service system for all our clients.

It is the same as on commercial airlines. You can pay a lot of money and get a first class ticket — which means you get bigger seats, champagne and caviar. Or you pay less and you get an economy class ticket — your chairs are smaller and you must wait till the trolley comes around before you can order your meal.

How to grade our clients

The place to start this process is to decide five different grades into which we put our clients.

A+
A
B
C
D

Then, with your team (your A+ team), decide upon your own definition for each grade.

Rank your clients by various criteria — here are some ideas:

1. How profitable is the client?
2. Do you enjoy working with them?
3. Do they pay on time?

Those are just a few examples. You can decide your own list of criteria, then rank your clients by those criteria.

To download a spreadsheet that is pre-done for you, go to www.accoa.co.uk/thehighlyprofitableaccountantworksheets

Once you have your clients ranked in order from best to worst, put them into your various categories.

I recommend that you have a maximum of twenty A+ clients. These are your biggest and best clients. These are the ones that you are prepared to take out to lunch every few months and speak with or see at least once a month, hopefully more.

The D category are the lowest 20%. It is from this category that you are going to do some culling. Some of these clients either need to increase their fees so they can shift into the C category (or higher), or they need to leave you because they really are *not* worth the hassle.

Customer Service Packages

I could see Phil pondering on this topic.

'Customer Service Packages... hmm... well, Rudi, we treat all our clients equally. It doesn't particularly matter how much they pay us. But talking about first class and economy class in the airlines, I can see that by doing what we're doing, we're probably under-servicing our best clients, and over-servicing our worst clients. In fact, it is often the worst clients who are the biggest drain of time and energy!

'Okay, Rudi... so how do we tackle this one?'

Once we are clear on our categories and we have identified which clients are in which category, the next step is to create a *systemised* Customer Service Package for each of those grades.

The way to do this is to sit down and for each category, draw a timeline over twelve months and decide your *What*s and *When*s around their Relational Connections.

Again, this is completely left to you and your team on how creative you want to be on this topic. There are no rules. There are no rights or wrongs. It is completely up to you.

Perhaps A+ clients get a call from you (or the partner in charge of this client) once a month to discuss life in general, and business as well. Once every two months they are taken out for a meal at a fairly smart restaurant for which there is no charge to the client in any way. Once every three months they are taken out for a sports day/activity — either watch a game, or go out for a game of golf.

But at the same time we also want to decide the *What* and *When* on their Transactional Connections, because at the end of the day these people are concerned about their businesses and their finances and want an expert to explain to them in layman's language what is happening and where they could improve.

So these conversations/meetings also need to be timelined. Decide on how regularly they will be happening in your practice, with your clients. Reminders of these actions can be put into a CRM system/computer software so that there is an automated system in place to remind you and your team of these actions.

And decide this rhythm for each of your grades of A+, A, B and C. The D clients are the ones that you want to eliminate.

'And Phil — always remember that for every project you have, you need to have a project manager. So remember to pick your champion for this project to ensure that it gets implemented,' I reminded him.

And Phil's response was, 'Rudi, this makes complete sense to me. Again, I can completely understand where we went wrong. By implementing these two systems into my practice, they will make us almost 100% immune from attack from our competitors. These two systems will ensure that we not only have Transactional Connections with our clients, but it will also systematically ensure that the Relational Connections are in place as well.'

You got it, Phil!

When you implement these two systems into your practice, it will ensure that the honeymoon relationship that started at ten out of ten, followed by the gravity that will weigh it down over time, will be countered, resulting in maintaining your relationship at least nine out of ten for the life of this client.

And with a nine, it is incredibly unlikely for this client to want to go anywhere but stay with you.

2. Lock-Up and Cash Flow

The first time I met Josh at his firm, he was short of breath. His stress levels were very high. As a five-partner firm, they had been banking with Natwest Bank forever. But their overdraft had been sitting at just short of £1m for a long time — and they were running their business on that overdraft limit, never really reducing it much.

And the bank had become concerned about this. As a result, they were moved over to a division within the bank that looks after problematic accounts. This was a big blow to Josh's confidence. At the end of the day, as managing partner, this sat squarely on his shoulders.

And there have been progressively more and more months where they have had to battle to have enough cash for payroll.

They had about £1m in outstanding debtors and about another £800k in Work-In-Progress.

Josh was embarrassed about the situation they found themselves in — and if he knew how to get them out of it, he would've done so already.

Reality is that every one of the partners were overworked. Josh's inbox consisted of hundreds of emails and he was falling behind. And on top of that, there were a few things in his personal life that made his personal stress levels extremely high.

Here are some of the steps we took over the next three months in Josh's firm to completely turn things around.

Please do remember that the following may or may not be relevant to your own practice. Always keep in mind that you are looking for principles and ideas which you could in one way or another translate into your own practice.

Step 1: Current Outstanding Debtors

In order to reduce our Current Outstanding Debtors and get this under control, there are a few things we need to do.

The Terrier (not to be confused with the Guard Dog)

As with all roles in any organisation, we need the right personality to be doing the job of credit control. We need someone who is persistent, tenacious, friendly but assertive and confident.

Do *not* make the mistake of picking a receptionist who is running low on work to do this job if her personality is not suited to this work.

The person we pick needs to have sufficient blocked and focused time available for this role. If your debtors' book is sufficiently big enough that this is a full-time role, that is great. If this is a part-time role, then that person only needs to be focused on doing this job for certain blocks of certain days.

Every week.

Weekly Meeting Rhythm

When something in your world is not working, you want to increase the frequency of looking at that item. When my kid is healthy, I don't need them to take medication — *ever*. When my kid is sick, I want them to take their medicine three times a day *every day* until they are better.

The rhythm of catch-up is very important.

When our debtors' book has spiralled out of control and we have found someone to start chasing those debtors, then we want to put in place at the very least a weekly meeting of catching up to find out what the latest progress is.

You want your Debtors Control person, your 'terrier', to come into the meeting with a printout of the Aged Debtors Summary. Quickly review it with them, starting with the oldest column first. Work your way down that column for every material debtor (you decide which number you will choose as your materiality figure, otherwise you will need to stop at *every* debtor, and depending on the size of your list, that may simply take too long). For every material debtor the question is always the same. 'Give me in a few words only the *Who*, the *What* and the *When* (yes, it is our friend, that *ding!* triangle again). Who did you speak to? What did they say?' Keep this bit short. 'When are they paying us or when is the next step?' Once you've completed your oldest column, then you start at the top of your second oldest column and work your way down that one until you've made your way to the current debtors.

This process can be completed in less than twenty minutes. Quick, snappy answers.

Typically, what you will find the very first time you go through this list in this format is that your Debtors Control person may have very few answers, or that they want to give you *long* answers.

If you find this to be the case, simply say, 'Thanks a lot — good work so far. Carry on with this work and when we meet again in a week's time, I'll ask you the same questions again.'

Remember — we are in a process of puppy training once again. This is not about getting frustrated or upset. It is simply a way of showing what we expect to happen.

And what you will find the second time you do this meeting one week later is that the Debtors Control person will have worked their way through the entire list, and this time will be able to give you short and sweet Who-What-When answers for every outstanding debtor.

What you will *always* find is that once this process starts, money will start hitting your bank account by the thousands. Just reminding clients about their outstanding amounts will get a lot of them to take action and actually settle their outstanding invoices.

Now the clear-up begins.

All invoices that are on the ledger which need to be written off or corrected — set that as a task for the coming week.

Debt Recovery

What you will also find through this process is that there are some debtors on your books who have been there for a long time and are simply taking the mickey. Perhaps they are not clients anymore. Perhaps they always have fantastic, but nevertheless weak, excuses. These are the ones you need to decide to take to the next level.

At the end of the day you and your team have put in a lot of energy and focus to do the work they required. In a fair exchange, they owe you money.

But some are non-responsive.

Various options exist — legal firm, debt recovery agencies, small-claims court.

Whatever option you choose, the point is that you have to draw a line in the sand and take action.

This may require some courage, but as with all leadership, it is about doing the right thing, not the comfortable thing.

You have kept your side of the bargain, which is to do the work. Your client needs to keep their side of the bargain, which is to pay you.

You are not the bank for your clients.

Within four to eight weeks of implementing the above, your outstanding debtors will be in control and you will have cash in the bank.

Putting the systems in place

Invoice Due Systems

We want for our 'terrier' to put an Invoice Due System in place. This can take various shapes.

1. This may mean that one week before an invoice becomes due, the client receives an email reminding them that the invoice will become due in one week.
2. On the day when the invoice becomes due, they receive another email reminding them that the invoice is now due for payment.
3. One week after the invoice is due for payment, they get another email letting them know that the invoice is now overdue.
4. And one week later they get a phone call from our 'terrier' person, who then stays on their case until the invoice has been paid for.

Ideally we have a way to automate these email steps, but if not, then it can still be done manually.

Direct Debit

You want to start shifting your clients over to a direct debit system, as it puts you in control of when money is taken. More importantly, unlike standing orders, when there are extra amounts, or larger amounts, you are in control of getting the correct amount paid from your client. A fixed standing order figure will require a separate payment from the client once in a while.

And of course, this never means that you simply have an open cheque book with your clients.

Absolutely not!

Any amounts taken need to have been pre-agreed and your clients need to have signed their agreements to each and every amount that will be leaving their bank account. Never assume that you mentioned it in a conversation and at the time they nodded their head and said 'Yes.' I promise you that will only come back and bite you where you don't want to be bitten. Ensure that you always have your signed upfront agreements.

This will require a decision on your side to make this happen, and then a concerted effort to have this conversation with all your clients. You must let them know that not only is it in their benefit to pay their account on a monthly basis going forwards, but as a proactive practice, you are keeping abreast of times, and in the same way as they pay their electricity and phone bills via direct debit on a monthly basis, going forwards, that is how you will be doing it as well.

Will all clients move to this system?

Unlikely.

Is it a good idea to try and get as many of your clients to make this shift?

Definitely!

It will put money into your bank account — money with which you can either build your practice, or just go and have a great holiday.

We will discuss more on this system in the next section on the debtors system for new clients.

Are *all* your clients going to pay their outstanding debts as you'd like it to happen? Probably not. But the better question is, Are the *majority* of your clients going to pay their outstanding debts?

Yes. If you follow the system as outlined above, then they will.

And you will have much more cash in the bank.

Following this process, Josh and his team reduced their outstanding debtors by almost £525,000 in only four months.

Step 2: Debtors As New Clients

When it comes to putting a system in for new clients, this is the easiest thing to do. Because they have no history with you. They are in the honeymoon phase. And they'll follow your guide on 'This is how it is and this is how we do it.'

With that in mind, some of the systems we want to put into place are as follows:

Direct Debit

When a client is not on direct debit, we are essentially leaving it up them to pay us when it suits them. Then it costs us to pay someone to chase them for their money which is rightfully due. Paying someone to do this task is another way our profitability can be impacted.

Direct debit outweighs standing orders, because with direct debit we have the ability to change the figures (next year's increased fee, which they've agreed to, needs a change on the monthly paid amount). Where extra work has been completed, we have the ability to take that money as per our agreement with the client.

Direct debit puts you in control.

I would highly recommend a system such as www.GoCardless.com. It is very easy to set up. It costs, at the time of writing this book, 1% of the transaction fee with the maximum amount being £2 per transaction. Which is fairly inexpensive.

The idea is that your clients spread their costs over ten or twelve months... and that they will have paid your fee before you actually do the work.

This system will cause you to end up with negative debtors.

Upfront Agreements

This next piece is really important — make sure you have pen and paper and that you are making notes!

There is a concept known as the 'Call Girl Principle'.

I learned this concept from an American trainer. When I was writing this book, I had serious doubts in my mind on whether it would be appropriate to put this concept into a book such as this. But it does illustrate the point really well, so *upfront* I'm asking for your forgiveness — and to bear with this story.

The Call Girl Principle states that the value of a service delivered is at its highest value *before* the service has been delivered. *After* the service has been delivered, the value dwindles very quickly.

That's it. That is the principle.

Am I forgiven for using that as a story?

Hopefully.

This Call Girl Principle on service delivery definitely holds true for the service that accountants deliver as well.

Before we deliver our service to our clients (getting accounts finalised before deadline dates and penalties, getting tax returns in on time before penalties, delivering a special project, etc.), our service has the most value (because our client is essentially, at some level, in a state of desperation — there is a deadline and penalties are not nice... please, please, please get it done!).

Once the service has been delivered (and the client is no longer desperate), then the value of the service dwindles very quickly.

Which means that when the client gets an invoice two months later and six months after that, they eventually take out their cheque book to pay you, but the following conversation might be going through their head: (in *that* tone of voice...) '*How* much? For *what*, exactly? This darned accountant of mine sees my financials and he's just taking me for a ride. I can't believe I have to pay this much. What a rip-off! I'm going to call him and get this invoice halved. This is ridiculous!'

And so merrily, yet again, you hit all of your write-off targets.

Well done, you!

The implication of the Call Girl Principle is that you want an *upfront* written agreement with your clients on:

1. Exactly what you will be doing for them,
2. How much it is going to cost them,
3. Exactly how and when they will be paying you,
4. And for any additional work outside of the scope of your agreement there will be a separate work order for which they need to sign before that work will be done.

This upfront agreement needs to be signed to indicate that they are happy to continue.

Once you have the abovementioned system in place, your cash flow will start improving because for every new client signing up, they'll be paying you in advance of their work being done. Profitability will improve because you have a system in place that will take care of scope creep.

Step 3: Improving Work-In-Progress Days

Work-In-Progress (WIP) is another culprit where hundreds of thousands of pounds can be sitting elsewhere instead of our bank account.

Let's take a look at WIP. There is a point where the work enters the system. We then bill time against the job. At some point the job is complete and we can invoice it. When it is invoiced, it moves out of the WIP system into 'debtors'.

There are many reasons for WIP to be high, but two major reasons are:

The work has been sitting on our 'factory floor' for ages and it is just piling up, not getting completed and invoiced. There is a bottleneck inside of our factory.

The work that is on the factory floor, for which we had an original budget for let's say £2,000, is sitting at £3,850 and we're still not finished with the job. We all know that for most such cases, this high WIP is also going to lead to high write-offs.

If only we could take control of those two biggies... right?

Here are some possible ideas.

1. Taking control of work sitting on the 'factory floor'.

This is a project in its own right. When you decide to start this project, it needs single-minded focus until it is done. Starting it, letting it slip, four weeks later picking up the pieces again... that is a process that leads to failure.

When you are on it, stay on it until it is done!

In order to reduce WIP, what we really want to be tracking is turnaround time. To do that we need three numbers.

1. Date started
2. Date completed
3. Number of days in the factory

You can easily get a receptionist or admin person to do this task for you on a simple excel spreadsheet and to report it to you on a weekly basis.

Once you have the average number for how long work takes to be turned around in your 'factory', the next open-hearted dialogue with your team is, 'Hey everyone. That is a great starting point. But it is really way too high — and, quite frankly, unacceptable. How and what do we do differently going forwards to push that down to X days?'

Have a dialogue. Throw ideas around. Get everyone involved.

Then implement the ideas that come up from that conversation.

Keep tracking actuals against your target number on a weekly basis, with continued dialogues with your team. And keep pushing on this until your target has been achieved.

Be relentless!

2. Billing is over budget, which leads to write-offs

It is obvious that it is really important for our *Who* on a job to have a clear budget for that job before it starts — this is expressed in hours as well as pounds.

Let's keep this example simple.

To get Job X completed, it should take Sally four hours, plus one hour of manager time, which equals five hours to get job done. 4 + 1 = 5. Simple.

Ideally, that plan needs signing off by a superior *before* we start the job.

Let's agree on some milestones along the way. And let's start using exception reporting.

In other words, if you are halfway through the job and it is in line with half the £ budget, then keep on going.

If you are halfway through the job and you are off course by more than 10% compared to £ budget, report it immediately so that corrective actions can be taken.

If action is required, questions to ask might be, 'What can we do differently in order to achieve our desired result within budget? Do we need an early conversation with the client pointing out that we have come up against some obstacles which will be pushing the budget up, which the client needs to agree to? Do we need other people involved on this job to push it through within budget?'

And sometimes there is simply nothing we can do at this stage to change the direction of the outcome. But then we can ask ourselves, 'What do we change on our side in order to avoid this from happening again in the following year with the same client?' If required, adjust systems company-wide to eliminate and avoid unnecessary errors.

Having a write-off in one year can be overlooked. But to repeat the exact same pattern in the following year? Well, there is no real excuse for that one!

At the end of every job where it has exceeded the target billing, we have to enter into an open-minded, inquisitive learning phase.

With the team on the job, let's agree that it went over budget, and also let's:

1. Figure out the reason for why the job went over the target, and
2. Put a system in place to take charge of that specific reason in order to avoid it from recurring in the future — both for the company as a whole and especially for this specific job.

An objection I've heard some partners raise is, 'Rudi, we've tried that before and it doesn't work. Staff would work overtime and simply not bill the time against the client because it looks better, but then we have people who are putting in long hours and not getting recognised for it.'

Remember that it is important to enter an open-hearted dialogue with your team on this matter. You are together looking for answers to make things better and more efficient. You'd rather them be completely honest and bill all their time.

That way you can gain clarity on which jobs we are being ineffective on and then work out together with your team if:

1. Perhaps they need extra help and training, or
2. We've genuinely underquoted the client and we need to have a conversation with the client about this for next year, or
3. We need to find a different approach on this job to ensure it comes in under target going forwards.

One key phrase you may have noted throughout the above was 'together'. Remember, you have an A+ team! You and your entire team are in this together with the purpose of ensuring that the practice as a whole becomes better — in every way.

If you persistently ensure this happens, in a matter of only a few months your team will have gained enough learnings and implemented new systems that soon enough, write-offs will become a thing of the past.

Making mistakes — that is okay.

Ignoring mistakes, and not doing something to avoid the same mistakes in the future — that is *not* okay!

Depending on your personal circumstances, you may choose to bring a rule in place to let all clients know that once WIP on a job reaches £X amount, the work will automatically be invoiced up to that point in time — which may mean more invoices for smaller amounts and therefore additional smaller payments... but it will definitely assist your cash flow situation.

Putting the above in place does require your leadership to be strong.

To be assertive. To be persuasive. To be persistent. To keep on pushing with the changes until it has been implemented.

As a result of the changes above, Josh's practice completely changed. Their cash flow became positive. The bank moved them out of the 'problematic accounts' division. They went on to acquire other practices and scaled much bigger. Josh's confidence levels went back to normal. And his stress levels...reduced to Zen-like calmness.

3. KPIs

One of my clients, Jonathan, was managing partner at a ten-partner firm. Things were going well for the firm, but one of the upcoming stresses for Jonathan and his partners was the imminent (five years away) retirement of senior partners. They must ensure not only 1) that there was enough money in the coffers to pay out their retiring partners' capital accounts, but 2) that the legacy left behind for upcoming partners was in fact a great business to be proud of.

As we went through the gradual process of implementing systems, eventually I asked the question on whether or not, and how, they tracked KPIs.

Jonathan gave me a blank stare.

The problem was not the tracking of KPIs. They *were* tracking KPIs. But they were drowning in data. There were so many numbers, so many different divisions, so many partners and managers, that they may as well effectively *not* have been tracking any numbers whatsoever.

This is a huge problem. If you don't effectively track the *right* KPIs in your practice, you will find yourself being shrouded in a fog. You will have a sense that things could be much better, more productive, more profitable, but you can't quite put your finger on it. There is just this nagging feeling that you have...

But if you *do* track the right KPIs, you will know exactly where to make improvements and your practice will constantly get better — which will result in your becoming a very efficient, effective, highly profitable practice.

Having said all of that, I don't believe there is one set of magical KPIs that all accountancy practices should track. Depending on where you are in your development, you will want to track specific numbers to help you get over the next hurdle of where your practice is at the moment and that will help you move to the next level.

Also, I believe that there should be two separate sets of KPIs.

One for your practice as a whole.

One for your team members — perhaps as a group e.g. per pod, or, individually, e.g. per partner and per manager.

KPIs work when there is a target number which is then compared to an actual number at a set frequency — weekly, monthly, quarterly or even annually.

Business KPIs

Where do you want to push yourself? What are you *not* happy with?

- Do you want to increase your revenue?
- Your profitability?
- Debtors' days?
- WIP days?
- Your sales appointments?
- The number of referrals you're asking?
- New clients gained?
- Turnaround time?
- Customer satisfaction?
- Productivity?
- Recovery?

Those are just some ideas. Expand the list to include your own areas of improvement.

With our Blackbelt Boardroom clients, we ask them to track and submit KPI numbers each quarter for their practice. Often they begin by admitting they have no idea and have never even thought of tracking some of these numbers. But over time, as they put systems in place in order to track the numbers and work on improving them, the numbers start moving in the right direction.

Team KPIs

You definitely want to set targets for your team members and then measure actuals against those targets.

For team members, the recommended number of weekly KPIs to be tracked should be somewhere between three and five. This should keep it from becoming an unfocused set of data which starts losing meaning.

You want to track this per pod of team members or per partner or per team member — or all three. What is it that you want to improve? Where do you need to bring your focus that will help your practice improve its numbers?

Here are some examples.

Perhaps you wish to improve turnover? Or turnaround time? Number of customer-service calls? Number of referrals gained? Pick your three to five KPIs for your team members and start tracking them against targets on a weekly basis.

Whiteboards

One of the most powerful things you can do when it comes to KPIs for your team is to go and get yourself a whiteboard. Put it up on a wall. And then ensure that your team's KPIs and targets are written down on that whiteboard. Updated on a weekly basis.

This brings an immense amount of peer pressure to bear.

KPIs and targets that are hidden inside a computer somewhere where we can either see it on a screen or somewhere on a printed report are not anywhere nearly as powerful as numbers that are written up on a large whiteboard where it is in plain view for everyone to see.

One of my Blackbelt Boardroom clients, Alan, who has a practice on the South Coast reported that initially he was a little sceptical about getting a whiteboard to write the targets and KPIs on, but that he went ahead and did it. He found that it completely transformed his team's activities and actions as a result.

KPIs create responsibility and accountability.

And when that responsibility and accountability is in the public domain (within the office environment), it brings a lot of pressure to bear — which yields great results.

Now back to Jonathan.

Along with all the other systems Jonathan and his partners were putting in place, this was yet another piece of the puzzle that fell into place for them. And as they started doing some of their reporting per partner, it was quite clear which partners were weak performers on certain areas which needed improvement. Because the numbers per partner were reviewed on a monthly basis in a financial meeting, with the numbers clearly displayed up on a whiteboard against targets, the encouragement that was brought to bear as a result yielded significant improvement in both sales activities as well as WIP- and debtors'-days reduction.

4. Becoming Efficient Through Technology

It was in Spring, 2013, that I first met Michael. At the time, he was 32 years old, and his practice turned over around £400,000 per year. Michael is an interesting person. Definitely 'glass half-full' — or, more likely, 90% full. Bubbling over with enthusiasm and excitement. A real can-do attitude.

But like a lot of accountants, Michael had his fair share of (fairly normal) challenges: too many non-A+ staff members, unproductivity far too high, net profit margin of the practice sitting around 18% at the time... debtors' days at the time around 120 days, WIP days around 80. Michael was working far too many hours, which had a negative impact on his home life. He felt as if he was on the merry-go-round all the time, which caused his stress levels to skyrocket. And because of this constant busyness, he never quite had enough time to think clearly and make good decisions.

Even though Michael is a very positive person, he was deeply frustrated with where he was at. And he knew that there had to be a better way.

That was what initially prompted Michael to put in a call to me, saying, 'Rudi, not certain if you can help me, but let's talk.'

Fast forward 18 months.

Michael has made the jump onto the I step. He's reduced his staff numbers and now has a core team of A+ people. His profit margins are at 50% and climbing. Debtors' days are in the negatives. He has purchased his own office. He is on an acquisition trail, and last time I spoke with him he had just completed the acquisition on both an accountancy practice as well as a small legal firm. But the biggest bonus? He now has the time to spend enough quality time with both his wife and his young children. And he has regained a love for business. Michael has turned into a real *Monopoly* player. Financially, he is growing stronger by the day. But most of all... he is now living a life of choice.

A life of *freedom*.

It would be fair to say that in order for Michael to have made the jump from SE to BO and finally to the 'Investor' step, he implemented everything in this book. But in this chapter, let's focus specifically on the technology side.

When you get the technology right and working correctly for you and your practice, you will find that your efficiency will, at the very least, *double*.

Things move much faster.

You, your team and your practice all become much more efficient.

Because you're saving lots of time, you will also save lots of money.

Outsourcing is simplified. Your clients get results much faster. Which means that they are consistently happy and satisfied with your service. Which means that even more word-of-mouth referrals come your way.

And all of the above has a very direct influence upon your profitability...

...and, of course, your freedom!

In the following sections we will cover a number of concepts. It is up to you to do your own research within your own geographic region or country to find out what the latest and best solutions are for your needs.

Direct Debit

As already mentioned previously, a direct debit system is very powerful and crucial for cash flow improvement.

Paperless and Portal

Going paperless creates efficiency in that documents are all in one place (not on a shelf somewhere). It becomes searchable. It creates efficiencies.

Will it take time to implement and get used to? Of course.

Will it end up saving you lots of time and improving efficiencies down the line? Definitely.

Most providers who provide solutions for you to go paperless also provide a portal linked to their system (or you can get these independently). Having a portal implies that you will have no more (or very little) Royal Mail and postage costs, potentially saving you lots of money — which can be translated as *profitability* (and freedom — don't forget freedom!).

Without a portal, it means:

1. Someone has to print a document out,
2. Someone has to put it into an envelope and put an address on it,
3. Someone has to put a stamp onto it,
4. Someone has to get it to a post office,
5. Someone has to deliver the post after a few days,
6. Someone has to open that post,
7. Someone will most likely keep it in their in-tray for an undetermined period of time,
8. Someone will likely have to make a phonecall chasing the document,
9. Someone has to sign the document,
10. Someone has to put it in an envelope and put an address on it,
11. Someone has to put a stamp on it,
12. Someone has to get it to a post-office,
13. Someone has to deliver the post after a few days,
14. Someone has to sort the documents and ensure they get to the right place,
15. And finally... job done.

With a portal, it means:

1. Someone has to put a document into the portal for the client's signature,
2. The client is automatically notified,
3. The client logs into the portal,
4. The client checks and applies a very simple e-signature,
5. You are automatically notified that the signed document is ready,
6. And just like that — job done.

Does the second alternative seem a bit easier?

I think so.

Importing Data and Bank Statements

Bookkeeping and data input can be very laborious (read: 'huge negative impact on profitability'). And often, as accountants, we'd rather pass on this work because of exactly that. There simply isn't enough profit in it and too much effort involved to be worth our while.

But let's tap into that beautiful word: technology.

There is technology available which will allow you to scan documents and invoices. The scan is automatically converted by the software into a readable document, which can automatically be imported into an accounts' package.

We also have the ability to scan a bank statement. The software will automatically read it and post transactions that it recognises (the software will learn as it goes along) into the right accounts.

There are also direct bank feeds — which means the software links to the bank account and both directly imports the transactions and automatically posts the transactions that it recognises.

A lot of bookkeeping software packages will have bank feeds automatically built in.

What the above means is that the right technology will help you become much more efficient and eliminate a huge amount of unnecessary and expensive data capture.

This cuts time spent on the work, which increases profitability.

As Michael said, in the past, he used to turn bookkeeping jobs away because the profits on it were not worth the effort. Now he welcomes bookkeeping jobs with open arms because when they are done correctly using technology, there are huge profit margins to be gained.

Online Bookkeeping Systems

We all know that online bookkeeping is winning ground. Sofware like Xero, Quickbooks, Kashflow and several others are gaining more and more momentum.

Like it or not, it is the way of the future.

The benefits to you and your clients are:

- You will be seen as a trusted advisor. Which means that you will have access to your clients' financials on a much more regular basis, and can therefore be seen as a trusted advisor to them throughout the year, instead of just when you meet up with them.
- It enables added-value services. Whilst Cloud accounting often simplifies some of the compliance work, it enables you to use services such as Crunchboards to offer added-value services.
- It improves practice efficiencies.
- It attracts new clients. A lot of business owners are adopting Cloud accounting themselves, so they will be looking for accountants who are familiar with it and can do it for them.
- Clients can have peace of mind. Because all their finances are being updated and managed by you in the background, they can relax and focus on their business.
- It increases security. With everything in the Cloud, if your client's computer breaks, or their offices burn down, all of the data will be secure online.
- Keeping up with the times. Times are changing, and if you want to compete and thrive then you need to keep up with the times!

On top of that, something like Xero working papers creates huge amounts of efficiencies and time savings which again translates into profitability.

How to Implement Technology Effectively

You've made a decision — it is time. You and your team are going to implement some or other technology system which once and for all is going to completely change your lives.

Great!

But before you start, here are a few fundamental rules which would be really good for you to take notice of.

1. Never underestimate the magnitude of implementing any bit of technology.
2. Consider it to be a project for which you will use the Octopus Project Management system — which means that you have a project manager responsible for it... not you!
3. Definitely use the Who-What-When approach (see earlier chapters) with specific focus on the *When* around clear milestones.
4. Be patient and allow time for both implementation and integration.
5. *Pick one* project and focus intensely on it until it is done.

I recently spoke with one client who has been slowly trying, without any real success, for the past two years to implement Xero.

Because it is a project which was allowed to drift, it has created a lot of open and unfinished loops. This teaches our team that the leader is not serious about actually completing things. Which most likely has all kinds of other subtle, yet negative, impacts.

There is this thing, this project, that is robbing us of energy. Because it is not complete, with no real plan for completion, it is hanging over us, constantly sucking more and more bits of energy.

And when you have two, three or more open projects like that, you will be stuck on a treadmill of losing energy on those open projects.

Let's take the other extreme of this, and get back to our client, Michael.

Michael is super focused. When he starts a project, he is on top of it like a rash until it has been completed. When he made a decision to implement his online software, an extraordinary thing happened. The story I'm about to share with you is true, but it is unlikely that this will ever be repeated again. It is merely a valuable lesson, so pay attention.

Purely by chance, Michael was at a conference where he met up with the CEO of a well-known online bookkeeping software company. The two of them had a bit of a banter, but it ended up with a dare.

The dare went something to the effect that if Michael could get 150 of his clients onto this online software within a period of 30 days, the CEO would buy him a car.

Which car?

Well, since this was nigh on an impossibility, they shook hands on a Maserati.

For the next 30 days, Michael very intensely focused all his energy on getting his clients transferred to this online software.

The conversations with his clients were interesting — and essentially went along the lines of 'This software is fantastic. You have to. We're doing this. You're spending money on your current software, in any case, and actually this is going to be much cheaper. Trust me. You *have* to do it. We're doing it!'

With such strong intention and influence, guess what his clients did?

Within a period of 30 days Michael did in fact manage to transfer 150 clients onto this package.

Which is completely unheard of — a record had definitely been broken.

And to his credit, the CEO kept his word. Michael is still driving his Maserati today.

Like I said, I don't think that is an offer that will *ever* be repeated to anyone else again.

But there are learnings points:

1. Decide on your technology to be implemented.
2. Bring intense focus to it.
3. Get it done.
4. One project at a time.

Michael implemented all of the strategies above, and more. He has made the jump onto the I step. And his practice is highly profitable whilst he has time for himself to live the life of his dreams.

Using technology can make your practice very efficient.

And highly profitable.

Welcome it with open arms.

And take it one step at a time.

Towards freedom!

These were some of the fundamentals that Phil implemented in his practice in order to get the tick next to *Systems* on the Team-Systems-Growth Triangle.

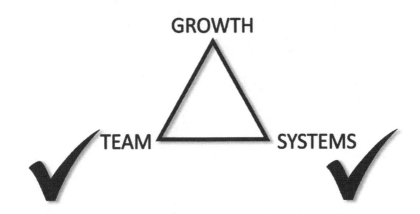

9. GROWTH

Once your foundations are properly in place, Growth is what is going to take you to that next level.

In the following section, we are going to take a look at some essential keys that you need to have in place to support your growth.

1. Getting the Pricing Right
2. Sales for Accountants
3. Marketing for Accountants
   a. Foundations Part 1: The Centre of the Spider Web
   b. Foundations Part 2: Spinning the Web
4. Selling Other Services and Acquisitions

1. Getting The Pricing Right

Phil had made massive strides in implementing a lot of this book so far in his practice.

Please remember that the order in which you implement the elements mentioned in this book will differ from one practice to another. It does make a huge difference for you in which order you implement it, so it is really important to get the order of implementation right for you.

On one of our regular coaching sessions, Phil brought up the topic of profitability within his practice. There was a lot going well, but he wanted to know how he could go about boosting his profitability.

So I said, 'Phil, I completely understand your frustration. Keep in mind, you've already done a fantastic amount of work in getting yourself to an A+ team, as well as implementing the right systems into your practice. You now have some very solid foundations in place that we can build upon.

'It is now time to look at pricing and what we can do there to directly influence your bottom-line profits.

'Phil,' I said, 'tell me about your systems, or your approach, to pricing?'

Phil responded, 'Well, it is fairly straight forward. I'll meet up with a prospective or current client and have a chat. Then I'll go away to do a quote. When I've done that, I'll email them that quote. If we're lucky, they accept. With our own clients, we aim for an increase of somewhere between five to ten percent each year for every client. Although that probably ends up being closer to five percent.'

Phil had a smile on his face. He'd learnt by now already that even though that has been his process for many years, there was probably a better way. And I was here to show him that way.

Phil said, 'Rudi, I'm guessing that in the next phase where you're going to help me with the implementation, we're going to be focused on improving my pricing systems? So let's get going. I'm ready!'

'Phil, you're quite right. And even though you began as my guinea pig in this process, you have risen to what I call the 'Blackbelt Boardroom' —

congratulations! And because I have since then expanded this process to many of my coaching clients, let me share with you a story of one of my other Blackbelt Boardroom clients so you can learn from what she did, and then we can decide on how we are going to get this implemented for you,' I said.

When I first met Elena, who is a very dynamic woman, she had had her practice for about three years. In those early days, despite the fact that one of her big differentiators was that she spoke Russian and offered an accountancy service for mostly Russian speakers in England, what she felt was her biggest differentiator was the fact that her services were cheap.

When she started out with no clients, she could afford to be inexpensive, as her overheads were very low initially. And then she managed to find herself some really cheap staff, so her services could still remain cheap.

But as a scalable model, for her, it wasn't really going to work in the long run.

As we started implementing systems into her practice, we eventually got to the point where we had to relook at her pricing.

The good thing for her was that one of the tools we use with our Blackbelt Boardroom clients is called a 'Pricing Maximiser'.

A Pricing Maximiser lists all of the services all of our clients sell, anonymously. Next to this list, there are five columns. Column 1 is empty. Column 2 contains the lowest of those prices. Column 3 contains the average of those prices. Column 4 contains the highest of those prices (which tends to be London prices). And Column 5 is empty, just like Column 1.

Elena then filled in her own current prices into Column 1.

To her surprise, Elena realised that, despite the fact that she was based in London, a lot of her prices were towards the bottom end of that scale. And not only that, but there were a lot of services listed that she didn't charge *anything* for.

Elena then started the job of putting her new, revised prices into Column 5. She filled in prices that were much closer to the level of other accountancy firms in London. And for some of Elena's prices that meant over 100% price increases.

With a lot of courage under her belt, Elena then, over a period of time, sat down every single one of her clients and had a conversation with them. The conversation went along these lines: in reviewing their accounts, she'd realised that over the last few years she had undercharged them quite dramatically. She immediately reassured them that what she would not do was go back in time and recover from them the amounts that she had undercharged. Unfortunately, she was unable to continue going forwards with those prices, and here were her new prices. If they were dissatisfied, then that would unfortunately mean the end of their business relationship.

Was that an easy conversation for her? No.

Did she experience self-doubt as she started out on this process? Yes.

Did it take courage? Yes — lots of it.

Did she lose a few clients? Yes — two.

Did she manage to increase her sales as a result of this exercise? Yes.

In fact, total revenue increased by 86.4% as a direct result of increased prices across the board.

So how do we get the pricing in our practice right?

Here are a few fundamental rules.

Stop Giving It Away

One of the biggest mistakes we make is that we give our knowledge away for free.

A client calls in and asks a question to find out if he should buy a new car in his own name or the name of the company.

The conversation could go in a number of different ways...

'Hi Janine. Business is going well and I've decided that I'm buying a new Porsche tomorrow morning. Should I buy it in my own name or the name of my company?'

'Hi Marcus. It would be best if you buy it in your own name.'

'That's great. Thanks, Janine. Bye for now.'

Or it could go...

'Hi Janine. Business is going well and I've decided that I'm buying a new Porsche tomorrow morning. Should I buy it in my own name or the name of my company?'

'Hi Marcus. Hey — that is fantastic to hear! It really does depend and there are a number of variables at play here. But if we get it wrong, it could end up costing you a few thousand pounds unnecessarily. We could do a Personal or Business Car Purchase calculation for you to determine which would be the best option. To do one of those would be £150. Would you like me to go ahead and get you one of those so you can know which will be the best option for you?'

'£150? Really? Well, I guess if it is going to save me a few thousand pounds, it is a bit of a no-brainer. Okay, yes please.'

'Okay, Marcus. I'll get a quick work order emailed through to you. If you can either sign it or simply email back that you are happy for me to go ahead and do this for you, then I'll start working on that for you straight away. All going well, you'll get the answer to your question before the end of today.'

That is just one small example. But when we start adding up all those small examples, suddenly it could make quite a big difference to your bottom-line profit.

When you walk into a supermarket, pick up a product, walk past the till without paying and out the door, do we call that 'customer service' or do we call that theft?

When your staff member gives a client your 'product' (their knowledge), and the client thanks them and walks out the door without paying, do we call that 'customer service' or do we call that theft?

Because in reality, how is that different from our supermarket scenario?

The problem, of course, comes into play when we haven't actually sat down and made a listing of what exactly all our products are.

Which means that you and your staff are merrily giving away your knowledge without realising that these bits of knowledge have a label on it. A label that says 'product'.

Your job is to sit down with your team and make a long list of every single thing that you have ever given away for free.

Then put a price next to each of those items.

And that becomes your product list.

Next step is to develop a bit of a script around how your staff approaches this the next time a client calls up and asks for a quick bit of free information. You could use or adapt the scripting between Janine and Marcus further up in this chapter as one way to do it.

Once the script has been developed, you need a bit of role-playing to ensure the team and yourself are confident in saying it.

And suddenly you are in a place where you can create an extra source of pure profits which, before, you were giving away for free.

Pricing Packages or Pricing Software

One of my clients who started working with us had a major headache. Both he and the majority of his clients were from an upbringing and culture where haggling and negotiating is the way things get done. Which is fine — but what he found was that more often than not, he would be haggled right into super low prices and essentially be doing a whole lot of work with very low profit margins.

Which was part of the reason that his net profit was in the region of 14%.

Which is definitely not the ballpark we want to be in.

So how did he end up not only dramatically reducing haggling over prices, but actually *increasing* his prices substantially?

Simple… productising and pricing software.

There are two ways to do this. And at the end of the day, they are going to give you a fairly similar result.

Step 1: Productising

We want to create a list of *all* our services, with a price next to each of them so we end up with a *price* list.

Once we have a written price for every single service that we sell, we have effectively created a Product List.

Now we are not selling services. We are selling *things. Tangible things.*

Step 2: Pricing Packages or Pricing Software

Next step is to make a decision on whether you want to create packages with some of these products included for a certain price. Or do you rather want to use pricing software which allows your client to pick and choose which products they want to have? This builds up a price as they go along so that they end up with a selection of products that works for them with a price that they selected.

Pricing Packages:

How do we create packages?

Well, do you want to fly economy, economy plus or business class? Do you want basic, basic plus legroom or do you want champagne with a fold-out bed?

You get what you pay for.

Whatever your seat choice… when you're flying from London to New York, bottom line is that you will get to New York, whichever way you select to travel on the aircraft.

Same with our packages.

I would recommend that if this is the route you choose, you create three packages. Gold, Silver, Bronze. One star, two star, three star. Name 1, Name 2, Name 3.

For each of those packages you can add a number of products, with the middle package being your optimum. The lowest package is the cheapest, but contains only the basics. The top-end package is the most expensive, but contains a premium selection.

We show our Blackbelt Boardroom clients exactly how to do this. But if you would rather do this on your own, then do your research. If you Google 'accountant websites that sell packages', you will see what others are putting into their packages and you can then create your own.

When it comes to selling your services, packages are the most simple for your prospects and clients to pick which service they want. It is a matter of picking the package that is best suited to their needs.

Pricing Software:

Here I would recommend that you look at something like QuickEasyQuote.com (QEQ). At the time of writing, the price for it was £30 per month.

You enter all your products into QEQ with their prices. You are also able to show prices that are X% higher (e.g. if you're working with a prospective client that you know is absolutely premium and definitely wants premium services which they would be happy to pay for).

When you are with a client, you'd show them your laptop, they'd go through the products you offer and decide which ones they want. As they select the products, the price is shown on the side and it gradually increases as they add more. That way, they can add or remove products as they go along.

And when you get to the end of that exercise, it is very clear to them what they'll be getting and what it will cost them. Which means you could email them the quote then and there, they could sign it...

...and the deal is done.

So how did my client reduce his haggling and increase his prices?

He adopted QEQ. When he went to his clients with his laptop, the very fact that their prices were now being built for them on a computer screen as they were staring at it changed something in their outlook. When they started haggling, my client would say something to the effect of, 'It is not me... this is what the computer says. My hands are tied. There is not much I can do here.' Invariably, they would still haggle, but he would end up only giving away a maximum of £50 to £100 off his set prices.

On top of that, he made a decision that he would go through a price-increase exercise — any clients that thought he was too expensive, he'd rather lose, so that he could put his energies into clients that valued his products.

Result: most of his quotes were increased by between 80% and 100%.

Did he lose some clients? Yes.

Did he end up with clients that he enjoyed working with at *much* higher margins? Absolutely!

After discussions with a great many of my clients who are using both the above systems, we've come to realise that there is an intrinsic limitation with both package pricing as well as software pricing.

It would seem that when a quote is around £3,000 or less, it is okay to use packages or software. But when it goes beyond roughly £3,000, then it becomes better to use a different method of pricing.

And that is...

Value Pricing

Colin walked into a client's office intending on quoting them £3,000 for a job.

He walked out having quoted them £21,200.

And they accepted that quote.

What happened?

As with every bit of knowledge within this book, reading about it is one thing. Implementing it and mastering it is another thing all together.

Colin had made a decision that something he really wanted to focus on and master was getting his pricing right. With that in mind, he studied all the materials he could find on pricing. He practiced the scripts that we give our Blackbelt clients and he mastered the methodology behind it. He bought every single book he could lay his hands on and really focused on getting to know this topic inside out.

To quote Matt, who is a partner at a medium-sized practice, who recently said to one of his junior partners, 'It has *nothing* to do with how much it costs us, but *everything* to do with how much value the client *perceives* he is getting.'

On the face of it that is a fairly simple and straightforward statement, but...

Let's take a deeper look at value pricing.

As stated before, value pricing typically tends to work better for jobs that are £3,000 or above.

It requires you to step out of a mindset of solutions and prescriptiveness, of 'I know what the client needs', and into a mindset of inquisitiveness, genuine interest and childlike curiosity.

How do you do this?

By becoming a clean slate and then asking the question, 'Why?'

Ask that question repeatedly within the same conversation, but in different ways — because, just like in a mine, the more you keep digging, the more you keep going towards the core. And when you do that long enough, you will eventually hit gold.

Your job is to become the detective and get to the very bottom reason behind the purpose.

The true purpose of whatever it is that your client wants.

And once you know the *true* purpose, you must figure out with them: if they *don't* have this project in place, how much might it cost them? *Or:* if they *do* have this project in place, how much will it make them?

And you want a currency symbol in front of that answer! e.g. £20,000, $50,000, €300,000...

Let's use a simple example to illustrate this principle.

Our client needs a mortgage certificate.

You could perhaps simply do it for free...

Or you could send the client an invoice for the service after you've done it without discussing it beforehand (which would probably get them infuriated for the cheek you have for charging for this)...

Or you could use some of the principles outlined towards the start of this chapter.

But to illustrate the use of the 'open slate' and the 'Why?' question, let's say our client's name is Dave. And Dave wants a mortgage certificate. I pick up the phone and I call Dave.

'Hi Dave. How are you doing? Fantastic. I see on my desk there is an application for a mortgage certificate. That's interesting. Tell me, what's happening in your world?' *(open slate)*

Dave: 'We're moving to a bigger house.'

Me: 'Fantastic news. So what happened that you've made a decision to move to a bigger house?' *(Why?)*

Dave: 'Ah, we just want one...'

Me *(Why?)*: "Interesting. So what made you decide that you want one now?"

Dave: "My wife is pushing for a new house."

Me: 'Really? Yes — that can happen. So what's going on that she is pushing for a new house?' *(Why?)*

Dave: 'Well, the kids are going to start school soon and she wants to be closer to the school for them.'

Me: 'Yes, I totally get that. Which school is this, Dave?' *(Why?)*

Dave: 'Ah, it is Queen's College.'

Me: 'Okay — yes, I've heard of them before. A really excellent choice of school, I believe. So Dave, how important is it to you and your wife to make this move?' *(Why?)*

Dave: 'It is really important. She's threatened me with my life if we don't make this move!'

Me (laughing): 'Ha… that's funny! It's probably not quite that extreme, but I can hear that it is clearly important.'

Dave: 'Mate, I'm not joking! She's complaining that I am spending too many hours at work and not enough time with the family. And she has seriously threatened that if this doesn't happen before the next school term, that she'll divorce me. This is serious stuff.' *(We've hit gold!)*

Me: 'Oh, gosh… sorry, Dave. I didn't quite appreciate the situation.' Let me just check that I understand this correctly. You want a mortgage certificate because you need that in order to buy the house you really want, which is close to Queen's College, before the new school term starts. And if it doesn't happen, your wife has threatened you with divorce because she feels that you are spending too much time at work and too little time with the family. You think she may actually be serious, so you have to get this sorted. Is that correct?' *(Confirm understanding.)*

Dave: 'Yes… that's pretty much it.'

Let's take a look at what happened there.

Had I done it for free — no profit.

Had I done it and sent Dave an invoice afterwards — he may very well have grumbled about having to pay for it — even refused to pay! — which may have led to a completely unnecessary deterioration of our relationship.

Instead, I called him up. With a completely clean slate with no expectations, no solutions, just pure, innocent, childlike inquisitiveness, I asked, 'Why?'

And I kept on digging and digging and digging until I got to the *core* reason of why he wants this.

Now that he knows that I care enough to have gone to the core reason of what is going on in his world, can you see how price now becomes almost irrelevant?

At this stage of the game, if I tell Dave that these certificates cost, say, £150 to compile, he may grumble a bit, but chances are pretty good that he will take it with a smile.

Or we can take the example of a business owner, let's say it's Dave again, who needs a cash-flow projection for the bank.

Again — we could do it for free. Or we could bill by the hour and at the end of the job hope that Dave is happy with the invoice and pays it without any grumbles.

Or we could try the 'Why?' approach.

'Hi Dave. Great to hear from you. So tell me, what is the reason you require this cash-flow projection for the bank?'

Dave: 'We need a loan and they need it for that.'

Me: 'Okay, I totally understand how they can be looking for a cash-flow projection for the loan.

Dave, how much do you need? But more importantly, when you have this money, what will it be for?'

Dave: 'We need half a million pounds. Just to make some changes to some parts of the business.'

Me: 'Half a million. Okay. So tell me a bit more... which parts of the business need changing?'

Dave: 'Well, it's like this. What we want to change is *(insert changes here... I don't want to bore the reader!)*.'

Me: 'Wow — that is all really interesting. So help me understand what your reasoning is for wanting to make these changes.'

Dave: 'Well, it is time to grow the business.'

Me: 'Yes, I definitely get that bit. So help me understand what has shifted. Why is now the time to grow the business?'

Dave: 'Because I've just turned 60 and I want my son to take over. It is time to take things to the next level so that when he takes over in a few years' time, things will be sorted for him.'

Me: 'Okay. So with these changes we are making to the business, what do you anticipate that will likely generate additional revenue for the business over the next ten years?'

Dave: 'Over ten years... well, I guess we'll be looking at adding an additional £10m over that time period as a result of these changes we want to make.'

Me: 'That is fantastic — well done! And if the bank is not happy with this cash flow, what happens then?'

Dave: 'Well, I guess we stand still, potentially even stagnate. And that is not an option, so we *have* to get this cash flow right so we can get this loan sorted!'

Notice that by asking open-ended questions with no particular agenda about where the answer is going to go, we've taken this from a very intellectual conversation to an emotional, from-the-heart conversation.

And when we get to the deeper reasons, our clients, both current and prospective, start moving out of being completely price sensitive.

And in the above conversation we are now also able to use the Contra Principle.

The Contrast Principle says that if we want to state a price, whatever price we initially give, all on its own, will always seem high. For example, sign up to a course and the course costs £500. That price is out there in the open all by its lonesome self. We have nothing to compare it to. And because it is all by itself, a part of our brains goes, 'That is the first price that I've seen... it is probably too high!'

But if we first paint a picture of how that course is normally valued at £1,000 and all its competitor courses are charged at £3,000, and then only after we've painted that picture do we mention that this course is £500... suddenly, in comparison, the course now seems like a bargain!

The Contrast Principle requires you to mention two figures: one large, and then your much lower figure. In contrast to the large figure, your figure now seems much more reasonable, doesn't it?

Which means that we could say:

'Getting this cash-flow projection completed on time in such a manner that the bank is happy with it means that in the next ten years you can potentially add £10m to your business.'

We've now moved away from 'We're going to work for five hours at £X per hour and therefore the bill is going to be £Y', and instead we can start a value-pricing conversation.

'By getting this project done in time so that the bank is happy to lend you the money, it will enable you quite reasonably over the next ten years to add £10m to your revenue. Our price for this cash flow project will be £X (pick a figure).'

To master value pricing takes time. It takes practice. It takes making a few mistakes as you go along.

But when you get it, when your confidence levels increase to such a point through sufficient practice that you are able to quote your value prices with confidence, always keeping in mind the genuine value your clients will get from the work you are delivering to them...

That is the time when your pricing will be at a truly optimal level.

And, strangely enough, as your own confidence and self-worth increases as you practice this strategy, so will the respect, the belief and the confidence that your clients and prospects have for you increase in tandem.

Phil realised that the next phase of implementation meant that he would need to make a decision to:

1. Stop giving his services away for free,
2. Decide his new prices for *all* of the services his practice offers,
3. Develop his own pricing packages or sign up to something like QuickEasyQuote.com,
4. And start using value pricing much more.

Of course, this project, as with every other project so far, does take dedication and focus.

But Phil stuck with it, and throughout his progress, whenever he'd reach a stumbling block we'd look at ways for him to overcome. And sure enough, within a matter of months, Phil had put everything into place and was noticing a very real increase in his bottom-line profits as a result of this work.

And, of course, an increase in his freedom.

2. Sales For Accountants

This is always an interesting topic for us accountants. I know that when I qualified as a chartered accountant, *none* of my training involved *anything* to do with Sales.

Nothing.

Zilch.

Nada.

In fact, my own concept of sales people was pretty negative and clouded. I thought that they were generally speaking born with the 'gift of the gab'. They were all extroverts, and I definitely wasn't. Honesty was probably not one of their strongest character traits. They probably didn't really have my best interests at heart, no matter what they said to the contrary. And I had to take everything they said with a pinch of salt.

Could I really trust a sales person? That would be a definite and resounding *No*.

Could I *be* a great sales person? Why in the world would I want to be like that? I had my morals and my ethics, after all!

And then I started my own business as a business coach and I soon realised that if no one was buying from me, 1) I couldn't feed my children, and 2) the people whose lives I wanted to help change and make better through the excellent service I was delivering, I couldn't get to, because if I couldn't sell, then they couldn't become my clients — which meant that all the technical knowledge I had to help them with so they could create much better businesses that could be their key to real freedom? They simply couldn't access that.

So for me, it became a journey of discovery to find or create a system which:

1. Was completely open and honest,
2. Would keep my morals and ethics intact,
3. Was completely transparent,

4. Created a win-win whether it became a match (a sale) or no match (no sale),
5. And it had to be a system that I or anyone else could follow that would allow the buyers to get to a place of making the decision whether moving forwards was right or not — and that we both were completely comfortable with that process.

So here is the system that took me many years of learning from a great number of different sources, a lot of trial and error to put together which, when it is applied correctly, can give you a 90% conversion rate on your qualified prospects (even if they came from cold sources other than referral)!

Phil's Sales Story

It was a Wednesday afternoon. 2pm. Phil came onto his Skype coaching session and we started reviewing his last few weeks and the progress he was making.

But Phil had only one thing on his mind.

Something that had really, really irritated him.

He had recently started doing a cold calling campaign and through that, an appointment was arranged for him with a business owner who had his own pharmacy. Phil called into the pharmacy the previous morning — their appointment was in the diary for 11am. He arrived at 10.50.

The pharmacist was busy serving customers behind the counter. When Phil got to the front of the queue, the pharmacist looked over his glasses at Phil and said, 'It is a little busy right now, but that is okay. I'll give you ten minutes. What's your pitch?'

Phil then mumbled and fumbled for those ten minutes. The pharmacist looked down at him over his glasses, thanked him for his time and said he'd be in touch.

As you can probably guess, this pharmacist never did become a client of Phil's.

Have you ever been in a situation similar to that?

Well, reality is that Phil made every Rookie 101 mistake in the book with that appointment.

So let's take a look at what makes a stereotypical second-hand car salesman.

(Upfront I need to make a sincere apology, because I know there are plenty of very honest second-hand car salespeople. I am purely using this industry and this stereotype as an example here.)

Let's take a look at how we can follow a system that will take us in completely the opposite direction of that stereotype.

In order for a sale to happen, there are a number of steps that we need to go through.

The steps are:

1. Know
2. Like
3. Trust

Do I know you? Do I like you? Do I trust you?

So let's take a look at our sleazy second-hand car salesman.

Do I *know* you?
He comes up to you with this huge grin that goes all around his head and stretches to Canada on the one side and Mongolia on the other side. A whiff of cigarette smell still hangs in the air around him. And he has this bear of a handshake that makes you feel like you truly are the long-lost friend from his childhood.

Do I *like* you?
He pulls you close to him and puts this bear arm around your shoulders. Now you are supposed to know that he is holding you close to him and everything in the world is going to be fine — because he has *just* the car for you.

Do I *trust* you?
He shows you this gleaming car. Opens the bonnet and it is absolutely *spotless* all over the engine. You wouldn't for a second think this is a second-hand car. And of course, there was only one lady driver owner

before. And you wouldn't believe it, but she was 74. And of course this car has only done 5,382 miles over the last ten years.

Oh boy, that nagging feeling in my head called intuition...

Now for Pavlov's dogs.

The dogs were trained. A bell rings... and the dogs start salivating. Whether there is food or not is completely irrelevant. A neural pathway has been created. A trigger starts the pattern, and the dog has to end the pattern by salivating.

So for me, when I meet a sales person and they are smiling *too* broadly, the Pavlovian response kicks in and my body has a very negative experience. Because somewhere along the line I have learned what the behaviours of a stereotypical salesperson are.

And it is really off putting for me.

Let's take a look at Phil's pharmacist.

Did he *know* Phil? Not from a bar of soap.

Did he *like* Phil? Maybe, maybe not.

Did he *trust* Phil? No particular reason to trust him, was there?

Did the Pavlovian response happen for our pharmacist? Absolutely. Phil was put into a little box, into a category of 'salesperson here to pitch and probably rip me off.'

So let's take a look at how we can create a system which sends a very loud and clear message of the exact opposite of this stereotype.

'I'm a professional. I am true to my word. I have very high ethics. I am very transparent and honest. I am *not* a stereotypical salesperson. Let's see if we can get to an agreement that works for both of us.

And believe me — if this doesn't work for both of us, I'll be the first to say, "*No*, this is *not* a fit, it would be best for both of us if we part company".'

Again, we are going to go through the three steps:

1. Do I know you?
2. Do I like you?
3. Do I trust you?

At each step we are going to put steps in place and take actions that go against the grain of what the stereotypical sleazy salesperson would be expected to do.

As a high level overview, here are the steps:

Know? Do a quick intro telephone call.

Like? On the telephone, like a doctor, do a fairly quick diagnosis on *if* we can help them. If we feel that we can, then we can take it to the next level, which is a face-to-face meeting. If we feel we can't, we *disqualify*. Also, through this quick telephone call, we are able to determine if we like each other. Perhaps we end up *not* liking the person for whatever reason. Perhaps we feel that they are simply too arrogant for our liking and even if we could help them, we really don't want to — in which case, again, we'll disqualify them.

Trust? This happens during the actual sales meeting where we ask a lot of questions to really get to *understand* their world. Only if they feel that they can trust us because we have really *understood* their world, will the sale happen.

Intrinsic Beliefs

It is really important that you understand the concept of 'Intrinsic Belief'.

Let's say that I am looking to buy a new car. My decision is between a Mercedes, a BMW and a Tesla.

My Intrinsic Belief is that each one of those have good working brakes. Their safety belts definitely work. And their engines will work. Those are answers that are so built into the product, I am not even going to think of asking any questions about them.

When a prospect talks to an accountant, their Intrinsic Belief is that you can do the work they believe you should be able to do. You can save them tax. You can do their year-end accounts. You have a good relationship with the authorities. You will get their documents filed correctly and on time.

Know, *Like* and *Trust* has very little to do with answering Intrinsic Belief questions. They assume that you can do what they believe you should be able to do as their accountant.

Important Note: the sales process described here is aimed at sales to mainly individual business owners. When we sell to committees or tenders, it requires a different process.

Your prospective client's Intrinsic Belief about your abilities as an accountant implies that your entire sales system or sales process should be built around ensuring that the boxes around *Know*, *Like* and *Trust* are ticked.

The *technical* solutions only come later. Because at some level their Intrinsic Beliefs are assuming that you will be able to supply them with great technical answers.

So let's take a deeper look at each of the steps and how we go about going down the route of Anti-Stereotype.

Referrals are always fantastic leads to have because most of the time they will convert. But even so, I would recommend that you create a system for yourself which you can follow each and every time, and then *use* that system, irrelevant on whether it is a completely cold prospect or a warmed-up referral prospect.

Step 1: Do I Know You?

Always ensure that you put in a quick intro call to your prospect, whether they are a cold or a referred prospect. Then arrange to have a twenty-minute telephone conversation with them to review *if* or *how* you can help them.

Consider the following:

'We don't work with everybody, so I'd like to get to understand your situation a bit more to see if I can help you and if we have a match. If we feel that perhaps I can help you, then we can take it to a next level of a face-to-face meeting to discuss *how*. And if we both feel that I can't help you and that we don't have a match, then we don't take it to the next level. Does that sound fair enough?

'Okay, so we're looking for about twenty minutes in our diaries. What is your diary like?

'Great! Also, before we speak on the telephone, I'm going to email you a brief questionnaire. If you could get that back to me before we speak, it will add a whole lot of value to our conversation.

'Great, speak with you then.'

So what happened here?

1. We did have a friendly smile, but it didn't exactly stretch from Canada to Mongolia.
2. We're stating upfront that we are professionals and not your stereotypical salesperson.
3. We are stating upfront that we do not work with everybody and that if we don't have a match, we simply won't take it further.
4. We are stating upfront that we respect time — both yours and ours.
5. Because we are clearly not acting as we'd expect our stereotypical salesperson to do, Pavlov's ringing bell will *not* activate salivation.
6. Our prospect is left intrigued, because they've most likely not ever in their life been treated quite this way during any sale... ever.

Step 2: Do I Like You?

During this part of the process, we are doing a diagnosis and, if relevant, a disqualification.

Bottom line: if we don't like each other enough, then this won't go any further.

We have a telephone conversation which goes something like this:

1. Very briefly, in less than four sentences: this is who we are and these are the amazing results we have obtained for some of our clients.
2. The purpose of this call is for me to ask you lots of questions to see *if* or *how* I can help you.
3. If I feel that I can't help you, I'll be the first to say so. And if I do feel that I can help you, then we can arrange another meeting to figure out exactly *how* I can help you.
4. Help me understand where you want to be ten years from now (turnover, profits, staff, hours worked, holidays, etc.).
5. Help me understand what is happening in your world at the moment (turnover, profits, staff, hours worked, holidays, etc.).
6. What would you say are the top three challenges standing between where you are now and where you want to get to, and what is stopping you?
7. You're talking to me right now and not your current accountant. What about them are you unhappy with?
8. To get this sorted, is this a sooner or a later thing for you?
9. Let me repeat back to you all the things I believe you've just told me.

If you then feel you have a match, you like this person and that you can help them, you say:

'At the beginning of our conversation I did promise that I would ask you lots of questions. And I did say that if I felt I could help you, I would say so. And if I couldn't help you, I would say so too. Well, the good news is that the challenges you mentioned are exactly the things I help my clients with. So shall we arrange a date in our diaries to meet up and go into much more detail *how* I can help you?

'Great!'

So what happened here?

1. We are stating upfront that we are professionals and not your stereotypical salesperson.
2. We are stating upfront that we do not work with everybody and that if we don't have a match, we simply won't take it further.
3. We are stating upfront that we respect time — both yours and ours.

4. Because we are clearly not acting as we'd expect our stereotypical salesperson to do, Pavlov's ringing bell *has not* activated salivation.
5. In twenty minutes we have probably gained more of an intimate understanding of this person's business than most other people may get over many years.
6. This builds immense trust.
7. The process is very transparent and honest. We are being very genuine when we say that if we cannot help them, we will say so. And they know this.

This process is not at all about our self-interests. It very much is about theirs. About genuinely understanding what is going on in their world. Listen carefully in order to make a diagnosis.

Step 3: Do I Trust You?

This is where we finally get to our face-to-face meeting.

By having taken the first few steps:

1. We have built our levels of trust,
2. It is very clear to our prospects that we are not the stereotypical salesperson,
3. We have made it clear that we actually do have their best interests at heart because we have asked a lot of questions and listened,
4. We have established quite strongly by now that if we do not have a match, we are absolutely prepared to walk away,
5. Because we have had a number of touches over a period of time, that has further helped to build our connection (our Relational Connection, even!) and trust.

Keep in mind that the main question to be answered for our prospect is, 'Do I trust these people more than I trust my current accountant? Do I trust that they know and understand me? Do I know that they would be able to come up with some good answers? Can I trust my affairs (and my life) in their hands?'

Because only when the trust level is high enough, would this person consider buying from you.

Our agenda for this meeting consists of the following items:

1. The 'Why Now?'
2. The Result
3. The Reality
4. The Roadblocks
5. The How

1. The 'Why Now?'

'Before we get into it, help me understand... Why now? Why me?'

These are interesting questions, as right up front, they go straight to the crux of why your prospect is thinking about making changes. And why they're speaking with you. By answering these questions, they are verbalising what is bothering them — and why they should consider you and your services. So listen close!

2. The Result

'Ten years from now, if you had a magic wand in your hand, what would be your turnover, your profits, your staff numbers, your working hours, your weeks of holidays per year?'

This helps your prospect identify very quickly a destination. Why do they come to work every day? What is it that they are hoping to achieve in their business?

3. The Reality

'Tell me what your current numbers are. What is your turnover, your profits, your staff numbers, your working hours, your weeks of holidays per year?'

4. The Roadblocks

'I want to understand your biggest three challenges in your business, and for each of those I want to understand the impact on your business if you don't get those challenges sorted. More importantly, for each of those challenges I want to understand the personal impact it has on you if you don't get those challenges sorted.'

Remember, at this stage of the game, your job is to be an active listener. Note down everything this person says. By asking lots of questions, you are opening the relationship to a huge amount of trust.

This phase is not at all about the huge technical solutions. This is the *Trust* phase. Because at the end of the day, if we've only had a low-level intellectual conversation about some numbers, they are going to end up in a place of, 'I don't really know if I trust you. I have no real bonding with you. And I'm not really sure if I do want to change accountants after all.'

And that will be their thinking, even if you can come up with some huge technical solutions.

There is a time for everything… and this is not yet the 'huge technical solutions' time.

But what if their challenge is Marketing, and you don't know anything about that subject? It doesn't matter. Read again: your Job at this phase is to be an *active listener*. There is *no* requirement at this stage of the game to come up with *any* solutions.

If they say it is Marketing, go through the process.

'What is the impact on the business if we don't get that sorted? What is the impact on you personally if we don't get that sorted?'

Listen actively. If you don't have answers, that is fine.

When they've gone through this process of emptying themselves out of all their pains and the things that really worry them, you may come onto the question about their current accountant. Obviously, if they were extremely happy with their current accountant, they'd not be in this meeting with you right now, so ask them to tell you more. And then keep quiet, because they will start telling you all the things about their current accountant that are upsetting them. Which is valuable information for you to have, because it teaches you what *not* to do.

Once you've completed that and you both are happy that you have at least their three biggest roadblocks or challenges and the impact each has on the business as well as the impact it has on them personally, then you go to the top of your scribbles and you repeat to them everything that they've said so far during the meeting, from the top. Confirm with them that your understanding of their world is correct and check with them if there are any obvious gaps that you have missed.

Generally, they will either help you fill in some missing bits, or they'll agree with you that you have an incredibly clear understanding of their world.

And for most business owners, this point is quite an eye-opener. Because they realise that in little over an hour, you have managed to gain an incredibly comprehensive understanding of their world. Which most likely no one else has ever done before. And it is quite likely that their current accountant does not have this level of understanding.

With that their trust levels with you go up a notch to the next level.

Because someone who has the ability to ask such good, focused questions to gain such core information probably also has the ability to come up with the right technical answers.

The obvious needs to be stated here. If you truly are unable to help this person, now is the time to say so. And then leave. They will respect the fact that you have actually listened to them and that you have the ability to walk away if it is not a match. They will have a very high respect for your honesty. The whole point of this exercise is to be completely transparent, open and honest. If you can help, fantastic. If you can't, then walk away with your head held high.

5. The How

Next step is to turn the tables around.

'I've done most of the question-asking up to this stage. Let's turn it around. What questions do you have for me at this stage?'

Typically, the questions now will be 'How can you help me?' and 'How much does it cost?' Which then naturally flows into the next step of you either using pricing packages, pricing software or setting up next steps to ask questions and scope a value-pricing project. You can explain how you work and what the next steps are.

But whatever happens, do ensure that you book the next meeting!

The hard work that you have done through this process of building the *Know, Like* and *Trust* will pay off handsomely as you start using this process going into the future.

I recall many years ago introducing an accountant to one of my then non-accountant clients. We went together to see the client. The accountant completely ignored the process of *Know, Like* and *Trust*. He simply jumped straight into huge technical solutions.

And because he tried to shortcut the process, even though it was a very warm introduction and even though he had some great huge technical solutions, the client did not change accountants.

And Phil and his pharmacist? Had he followed the process of *Know, Like* and *Trust* as described above, the outcome may have been very different.

But full credit to Phil: after our conversation and coaching accountability, he focused on implementing this process, learning the steps by heart and continuously practising it.

And today? Today Phil is a professional salesperson following a professional sales process.

Phil's practice is growing very nicely, thank you... and so is his freedom!

3. Marketing for Accountants

Phil has done a huge amount so far within his practice. His foundations around Team and Systems were now solidly in place.

And he was ready to turn open the tap on lead generation.

Which I totally agreed with.

A mistake I see very often is that we have a bathtub that is full of holes. And then a managing partner will say to me, 'Rudi, all I need to fix all my problems is just some more clients.' We then go ahead and open the taps. But because of the holes in the bath, as quickly as the water runs into the bathtub, it leaks out through the holes.

Which is why it is so important to get those holes fixed first.

And once they are fixed, then, by all means, open those taps, and your bathtub will fill up really quickly!

Phil said to me, 'Rudi, I will be the first to admit that Marketing is not my area of expertise. Face it — we didn't learn too much of this stuff in our years of becoming experts in our chosen subject fields.'

And of course, he was right. For most of us, when we think of Marketeers (which sounds rather sinisterly similar to 'Racketeers',...), we hold images in our heads of very extroverted, very loud, and even, quite frankly, unsavoury people.

But apparently this stuff helps to get us more clients. So, grumpily, we accept the point that as much as we don't really want to admit it, there is probably something in this whole 'Marketing' idea.

But here is the rub.

If a builder comes and gives you a quote for a job, and you know nothing about the work, is there a risk that you could get ripped off? Yes.

If my mechanic tells me there is something horrible wrong with my car's engine and I don't know anything about car engines, is there a risk I could get taken for an absolute ride? Yes.

If I approach anything in life which I don't really know how to do, is there a (good) chance that I may be taken for a ride? Yes!

And, unfortunately, this is also true for the subject of Marketing.

Often, it seems like a matter of 'Let's fling some money at the wall and hope that something sticks.'

That was why I shared with Phil the knowledge that you are about to learn in this chapter, so that he could master the subject of Marketing and truly get the foundations fixed and systemised properly in his practice.

But firstly...

Some Basic Fundamentals

1. Marketing has nothing to do with being extroverted. Marketing has *everything* to do with systems. Build the systems around every marketing process, and then diligently follow those systems.
2. Most of what falls under the umbrella of Marketing is a long-term game. You are going to build the systems. And then for the next ten to what feels like a hundred years you are going to diligently follow those systems, week after week, month after month, come rain or shine.
3. The biggest key to effective marketing is *consistency*. Once you've got your systems in place, you are going to keep on and keep on and keep on with *no* breaks, repeating, and repeating on a *consistent* basis. The biggest error that weak marketers make is to have a *lack of consistency*. They have a bit of a spurt, then give up or get distracted. Six months later, a bit of a spurt again, then they stop for four months... and so on. That is not consistency.
4. Your job is to be the #1 #2. Every business person and his dog has an accountant (barring our start-ups). That accountant is currently #1. And they will sit on that perch until they mess up on something and our beloved business owner becomes a little agitated. Now with any luck, they get *really* agitated and they start looking out for a replacement. We want to be that replacement. The way we do that is to ensure that of all the

options, we have been in their awareness for the last number of years with our consistency and always adding great value through our marketing. They're aware of us. Over time, we've naturally built a certain level of trust. And when the day comes that it is time for them to part with their previous accountant, we are the natural successor. Because we ensured that we were the Top #2 in their awareness. We were the #1 #2.

Here is a graph that explains how consistent marketing works:

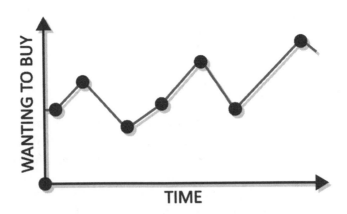

This is a graph over time which shows high points and low points in a person's needs. That timeframe could be an hour, a day, or a few years. My need could be for chocolate (once every 40 minutes during the day), or it could be for a holiday (once every three months), or it could be my need for a new accountant (once every... five years?).

The first graph shows the person's high and low need points over a number of years. The low point is when I am very happy with my current accountant and my need for a new accountant is virtually non-existent.

The high points are when I've just received an unexpected tax bill, or I am querying an invoice for something I don't think I should be paying for on my accountant's bill.

In the next graph, we can see a number of our consistent touches over time. It is clear that the place where we touch them (let's say once a month, or once a week) sometimes connects with them when they are absolutely *not* interested.

And sometimes it connects when they are *very* interested.

Our job is to consistently put great content value out there.

One day, they will become incredibly infuriated with their current accountant. Their need will be at an all-time high. And just on that day we will happen to be in their awareness again, with another contact point adding more value to their world.

We've done our jobs of:

    a.   Being the #1 #2
    b.   Being consistent.

They think to themselves:

    1.   These people have been sending me great value content for the last three years.
    2.   Their stuff is pretty good.
    3.   Oh, they are so *consistent*!
    4.   Let's give them a call to hear what they say...

That is when Marketing has done its job.

As with everything else in this book, it is always a matter of going back to basics. Get the basics sorted and properly in place.

Because when we have strong foundations in place, only then can we build a high-rise building on it.

Marketing: The Spider's Web

To understand marketing in a very simple way, think of a spider's web.

The first part we want to get right (Level 1) is to spin the centre of the spider's web. To get this bit done, it is all about putting in place and/or systemising the parts that we most probably are already doing – our website, asking for referrals, meeting up with introducers etc.

Once we are happy that the things we are already doing are in place properly and actually fully systemised, then only do we spin the rest of our spider's web (moving onto Level 2).

If I had to summarise in one word what the Level 2 spinning of the spider's web involves, the word would be 'Content.'

When people are seeking a new or different provider or solution, they are actively seeking for knowledge, or content. And when they do their research, when they speak to others, when they are on Google at 2am in the morning looking for answers, they are looking for content to provide them with answers to their problems.

Level 2, the spinning of the web, is all about creating content on a consistent basis, week after week after week. Content that will be of interest to your prospects. This could take the form of blog posts, webinars, seminars and more.

When you've reached the point where the centre of the spider's web has been spun and all the basics are good and they have been systemised and after that you've moved onto systemising the second part of the web with consistent content, then you will have spun yourself a spider's web that will work to a large extent without you. And it will work incredibly well.

Foundations Part 1: The Centre Of The Spider Web

Let's go through the *very basic* basics that we need to get right in order for our Marketing Machine to really take off.

You will need the following ingredients for this cake:

1. Your Marketing Team
2. Your Website
3. Your LinkedIn presence
4. Your Tactical Marketing Plan
5. Systemising your Referrals Process
6. Systemising Networking and Introducers

Your Marketing Team

First thing to keep in mind is that Marketing is a division of your business. Absolutely no point knocking yourself for the fact that you don't know anything about marketing. Quite frankly, you're not supposed to yet. You're the expert in another topic altogether.

But it is nevertheless a division of your business.

Which means that you need a team of people to help you perform this function within your business.

'A team?' you say. 'But Rudi, overheads are so high already, I can't afford to employ more people for this!'

I hear you. I heard Phil when he said the same thing.

But...

The bottom line is that we *do* need people who can help us do this.

So what do we do?

The answer lies in:

1. As with any other part of your business, this is a project — which needs a project manager. You are going to need to find yourself someone who can manage this for you. They can be part-time or full-time or outsourced.

2. Then we break down all the activities that need to happen into little chunks.
3. Next step is to put part-timers or outsourced people onto those different chunks.
4. All whilst your dedicated marketing manager drives it forwards and holds it all together.

Let's first take a look at all the different people we may need to fulfil the various jobs in our marketing team — and then we'll take a look at where you could find them.

1. Marketing Manager
2. Web & Online Specialists
3. Copywriter
4. Graphic Designer
5. Video Editor
6. Telesales
7. Partners & Managers

So let's take a look at each of those and what they are responsible for.

1. Marketing Manager

Keep in mind that this individual could be full-time, part-time or outsourced. Your marketing manager is responsible for deciding, with other senior team members (or you) the written Tactical Marketing Plan that we will be implementing for the year and which you will be holding this manager responsible for. Recruiting the right team members for this team.
Holding marketing team members accountable to their responsibilities.
Implementation of the ideas of the Tactical Marketing Plan
Arranging and coordinating events.
Yielding results.

Cost: anything from £500–£3,500 per month depending on how much time they are with you as well as their location.

2. Web & Online Specialists

Ensuring that you have a fantastic website.
Responsible for rankings and PPC (Pay Per Click advertising).

Responsible for Facebook and LinkedIn promotions/advertising.
Responsible for SEO (Search Engine Optimisation).
Landing pages and everything else online that will help you obtain a presence and lead generation.

Cost: anything from £18–£75 per hour. Ideally agree the cost of a project before it is started.

3. **Copywriter**

(Ideally your marketing manager is good enough at writing and can get involved with this task. But if not, or if your marketing manager doesn't have the time because they are working only on limited hours, then we'll need someone who can help us with this task.)
Writing copy for your website, landing pages, ads, blogs, etc.
Assisting with creation of lead magnets (short downloadable documents).

Cost: £8–£50 per hour. Ideally agree the cost of a project before it is started.

4. **Graphic Designer**

Making your presence look great with the right colours, designs, etc.
Helps with the great graphics and design for landing pages, lead magnets and anything else that requires a graphic designer.

Cost: £3–£50 per hour. Ideally agree the cost of a project before it is started.

5. **Video Editor**

When you get to the point of making educational video content, this person will come in very handy.

Cost: Approximately £30 to edit a 3–5 minute final cut video.

6. **Telesales**

These people have the ability to book you almost instant appointments and should be part of your team at some point or another. There is a full description on how to get telesales to work effectively in your organisation towards the end of this chapter.

Cost: Roughly £200–£300 per *kept* appointment.

7. **Partners & managers**

    These people are definitely part of your marketing team! They speak to prospects, they go to networking events and they are the people who meet up with future introducers. So yes — we *do* want them to report on their KPIs around their marketing activities and yes, we *do* want to hold them accountable if there is a lack of activities.

Where can I find these people?

Full-time: use the normal channels as described in the chapter on recruitment.

Part-time: you could use the same channels as described in the chapter on recruitment, or you could try a website like www.PeoplePerHour.com to see what you can find there.

Outsourced: you can use websites like www.upwork.com, www.fiverr.com or www.onlinejobs.ph.

Remember, you don't need all of these team members on day one. But as you go along, you may require services from all of them. And not a single one of them needs to be in full-time employment with you. It can easily be scaled as you grow.

Your Website

When someone finds out about you, chances are very high that they will take a look at your website. And first impressions do count. So why not make it good enough?

'I don't understand,' Phil said, 'Good enough? But shouldn't it be world-class, top of the range?'

'Well, Phil, it would be fantastic if you could do that. But the reality is that there is a minimum requirement. It is a bit like a pass mark in an exam. Let's say that pass mark is 60%. In other words, you can absolutely *not* get 59%. But 61% is good enough. 90% would be awesome, but 61% won't put people off.'

If I look at your site and it looks like it was built in the 1930s, I am going to find it off-putting and it will put a bit of a hesitation in my step when I approach you to be my new accountant.

So there is a certain point below which we cannot drop.

Then there is a point which is 'good enough'.

And then there is world-class.

If you are able to find a graphic designer who is good enough to help you create world-class, then that is absolutely fantastic. But at the very least you need someone to help you create a site that is good enough.

To get training on all of the elements that your website should have on it and specifically what I mean by 'good enough', go to www.accoa.co.uk/thehighlyprofitableaccountantworksheets

The elements that we require on our website in order for our site to be 'good enough':

1. Modern design
2. Language on the site that speaks to the pains of your prospects
3. Avoid technical jargon
4. Have great video testimonials
5. Have good photos of yourselves on the 'About Us' section
6. Ensure there are some downloadable 'bait' offers on your website

If you find yourself a fairly decent graphic designer and website builder to put those elements into place for you, you will end up with a website that is 'good enough'. A prospective client will take a look at it and they'll be happy enough to proceed.

We want to avoid and remove any unnecessary obstacles in the way that could stem from a quick glance at our website.

Your LinkedIn Presence

The next place a prospect may find your profile is on LinkedIn.

Again, we want to ensure that your profile is simply good enough, so as to not be off-putting to a person who is taking a casual 'Let me see who this person is' glance.

In order to ensure that your LinkedIn profile is 'good enough', we require the following to be in place:

1. Your name
2. A professional photograph
3. Your headline needs a good description
4. Your location and industry needs to be listed
5. You need a great summary explaining what you do
6. List your experience and specialities
7. List qualifications and certifications
8. Give recommendations to others
9. Ask for recommendations from others
10. Get connected

To get training on how to do the above, head on over to www.accoa.co.uk/thehighlyprofitableaccountantworksheets

Your Tactical Marketing Plan

As you'll know by now, having read this far in the book, in order to get results we need to set written targets, and then we need to track the actuals compared to our targets.

When we do that, we have a plan to follow.

And we can then compare how we are actually doing in comparison to our written plan.

A great way to do this is to pull together a spreadsheet that lists down the left-hand side *all* the activities we are planning on doing for marketing. Our columns are months of the year ('Plan' and 'Actual' for activities *as well as* 'Plan' and 'Actual' for results).

At the beginning of the year (or *now* if you are only just starting with it), set down all the planned activities per month.

As the year passes, each month record the actual activities performed. At the same time, also record the results from our activities.

Very soon you will notice patterns showing up.

And those patterns will — on the negative side — either indicate low activities or low results.

Which is great, because then we know what is *not* currently working and we can start fine-tuning or doing things differently.

Your marketing manager is responsible for completing the Tactical Marketing Plan.

This document also becomes the instrument you use to hold your marketing manager accountable — both for activities as well as results.

To get a free downloadable example of a Tactical Marketing Plan, go to this website:
www.accoa.co.uk/thehighlyprofitableaccountantworksheets

Referrals

For most of us, referrals are our life's blood. This is the one source from which, for most of us, new business comes.

And yet — for most of us — it is an activity that happens by accident.

Thank goodness! A client is happy enough that they've mentioned us to someone else, who then contacts us to come and see us!

So what might happen if we took this mostly accidental action and we put systems in place around it?

'What systems, Rudi?' you may ask, just as Phil asked.

Always keep in mind that getting referrals is a result of your 'spider web'.

If you currently only have one client or one referrer, you will potentially only receive so many referrals.

If you currently have 100 clients or 100 referrers, you will potentially receive 100 times more referrals.

The bigger your spider web is, the more you will catch.

When your web is hanging around in haphazard shreds, you will catch less.

When your web has systematically been spun, your chances for good catches — and many more of them — will be greatly increased.

Let's take a look at some ways of doing this.

1. On all your documentation:

The systematic spinning of your web here means that you bring the message of 'We are always looking for referrals' onto all of your documentation which your clients and contacts see.

Is it on your email footer? On your customer satisfaction surveys? On your regular correspondence? On your year-end agendas? Everywhere your clients could possibly see this message.

Why would you do this? Because you should be constantly planting the seeds about the fact that you are actively looking to improve many more people's lives, which means that they need to come and have a chat with you.

2. Using LinkedIn:

The method I am about to share with you, I give full credit to one of my former clients, Andrew Rhodes of Sobell Rhodes in London. Andrew is one of the humblest individuals I have ever met. He and his firm have over the years won almost every award in the UK accountancy profession, including Managing Partner of the Year, Best Medium-Sized Firm of the Year, Best Client Service of the Year, the WOW! Awards, the British Accountancy Awards... the list goes on. Andrew has for many years successfully been a very active member of BNI.

He is always striving to become even better at what he does — and I have a very high level of respect for him. I know that his firm does some training for other firms. If you ever have the opportunity to work with or learn from Andrew, then grab the opportunity with both hands.

Andrew refined and developed this method for generating leads via LinkedIn — and at the time, he was getting on average about 16 referrals *every* week as a result of this method. I recall him once saying to me that he had to switch this method off after a while as he was unable to cope with all the follow-ups as well as all the new business coming in through the door as a result.

What a great problem to have!

Here is Andrew's method in a nutshell.

1. Ensure that you have a 'good enough' LinkedIn profile (as explained earlier in this chapter).
2. Ensure that the connections you have on your LinkedIn profile are all people that you *actually* know.
3. You need at least 100 connections on there — both clients and general contacts.
4. Find someone in your client/introducer/referral list and ensure they have a minimum of 100 contacts on their LinkedIn profile (let's call this individual John Doe).
5. Call John and arrange a meeting whereby you will give each other introductions.
6. When you meet up with John, show him your LinkedIn contacts and ask him to whom he would like to be introduced.
7. Go through your own LinkedIn contacts with him and identify three to five people that he would be interested in meeting.
8. Send those identified contacts an email to the effect of 'Dear Mary. I'm sitting here with John Doe, who is a brilliant XXX. I thought it might be worth your while connecting with John. Are you open to receiving a call from him? Jack.'
9. Because it is a very warm referral, 80%+ of those contacts of yours will come back with something to the effect of 'Hi Jack. If you know this person and recommend them, then sure, why not? Ask John to give me a call.'
10. You pass those names on to John.

11. But at the same meeting where you send the email to your contacts, you swop around with John. And then you go through his list of contacts and you select three to five people that you would like to be introduced to. He too sends them an email stating that you are excellent at what you do and that it might be a good idea for them to touch base with you and *are they open to receiving a call* from you?

12. When John then passes his 'Yes' replies on to you, first step is that you put in a call to those people and have a bit of a chat. This is a 'disqualifying' step. For 50% of them, there will be no point in you taking it any further, and with those you simply agree to stay in contact for the future. But for the other 50% you will discover that it would make sense to arrange a meeting with them. Some of them will become clients at some point in the future. And some of them will become people who could potentially refer business on to you. And with those, you are going to repeat the exact process that you did with John.

13. Follow up with people and continue building relationships.

When you continue to follow this method in a systematic fashion, it will very quickly start opening doors for you.

3. Meeting up with clients:

Not all your clients, contacts and introducers are going to be active on LinkedIn. With these individuals, you arrange a meeting or a lunch. If they're a client, ask them to rate how happy they are with your services on a zero-to-ten scale, with ten being ecstatic and zero being really unhappy.

Whatever number they give you, say 'Thanks a lot. What could we do, or what needs to happen in order to increase that number by one?' And they will tell you. Take note of things they say — this gives you an opportunity to improve the systems within your practice.

The thing about this rating — if I go to a restaurant and afterwards I meet up with you and tell you that I've been to that restaurant, and as a score between zero and ten I'd give them a ten, what I'm really saying is: 'Do whatever you need to do, but go and try it out. It is absolutely worth it!' If I give them a seven, I'm saying, 'It was okay...' And a six or lower means 'Don't bother wasting your time or your money.'

So when you hear a client giving you a score of six or less, the message is that they are already looking for another accountant and they are on their way out. People with this level of scoring require extra immediate hand-holding and customer service to make them feel extra special so that the score can be raised as quickly as possible.

Unless, of course, you are trying to get rid of them — in which case, pat yourself on the back and withhold any further customer service.

Bottom line? Before you ask for referrals directly from clients, I'd recommend you ask them to rate how happy they are. If they answer anything less than an eight, it is not yet the time to ask them for a referral; firstly you need to fix whatever is wrong in order to get that number to an eight or above. Once it is there, then by all means, ask the question.

4. Track it:

You definitely want a spreadsheet where you can keep track of where your referrals are coming from over a period of time. This will highlight any persons or activities that you want to give even more special care and attention to in order to get even more referrals from those sources.

And you also want to keep track of the referrals you have given. Because if you realise that you have given a contact of yours ten referrals and they have given you none, then it would be time for a sit-down and a very serious conversation.

Networking And Introducers

These are further examples of spinning your web. Can these methods work? Of course they can. And they do.

Networking

Two types of networking environments:

1. You go to the same group week after week after week... this is all about building strong relationships for cross referrals.
2. An event where you know a few people which only happens very occasionally or even only once a year — here your purpose is to work your way through the room as quickly as possible,

ideally shaking hands with every single person, disqualifying the wrong people and taking the contact details of the qualified people with an agreement to call them the next day to take things further.

Let's take a look at the first environment:

Regular meetings with the same people.

Business Network International (BNI) is typical of this type of environment. The key here is to arrange meetings with the people you get to know in that room. Meet up at their offices. Show a real interest in them. As per the LinkedIn method above, agree with them to work together through cross referrals... and then start cross referring to them, with an expectation of the same to be returned at some point not too far in the future.

It is the strength of your one-on-one follow-up meetings and relationships outside of the actual meeting room that will make this a true success for you. Persistence and consistency is definitely the answer here.

Once-off events with a lot of unknown people.

Here your job is to have a fairly quick script which helps you either qualify or disqualify people in the room. Then you want to work your way through the entire room before the event finishes, having spoken with every single person there and collected the cards of all the people you have initially qualified in your one pocket so that you can follow up with them over the next few days to have an initial chat and to figure out if it is worth taking it further and meet up, either as potential clients or, more likely, as potential referrers.

Introducers

These are similar to all of the methods mentioned above.

Introducers you could meet through your regular networking activities. Or you could make a decision that, e.g., you wish to meet your local bank managers. It would then require compiling a list of these people, contacting them with a message saying that you are an accountancy firm and you could potentially introduce some people to them and you'd like to meet up. Very few introducers would be able to say 'No' to such an invitation.

Meet up with these people. See who you like the most and start passing referrals onto them. Keep track of cross-referral numbers — and then make a decision on which introducers you want to focus your energy on.

Then keep the relationship alive by regularly touching base, going for lunch and arranging for more cross referrals.

Phil's only comment after we covered the knowledge up to this point of the chapter: 'Rudi, the part we've covered so far, I'll admit that I probably do most of it already in some fashion or another. But you're right. Our web is probably a bit ad hoc and blowing in tatters in the wind as opposed to a good strong system. And no, I've not had a marketing team before like you've described it here, so I'll start working on that straight away!'

Phil jumped on it straight away and got back to getting the basics around marketing properly in place in his practice. In no time at all he found himself a part-time marketing manager to help him.

Foundations Part 2: Spinning The Spider Web with Long-Term Nurturing

When Phil had completed the basics, it was time for the next level in marketing.

And this advanced level is all about 'Content'.

'Phil, now that we've got the basics in marketing covered, the next step is the part where we take your marketing knowledge as well as your marketing engine to a whole new level. Here we are moving to the more advanced marketing methods. In order to get this part right, we want to spin the full web around us,' I said to Phil.

This part is all about building 1) lots of content, and 2) events where we can share that content, so that people who are hungry for information will look at us and think to themselves, 'These people are constantly putting really good, informative stuff out there. They really seem to know what they're talking about. I think I need to go and meet up with them.'

Obviously there are different ways to do this, and the methods outlined below take time to master, but ultimately, the rhythm and activities that you want running around this might look something like this:

1. Weekly blogs or videos
2. Monthly webinars
3. Quarterly (at least) seminars

Remember that the biggest killer of marketing is the lack of consistency.

So find a rhythm of activities for your practice to get content-sharing out there, and then stick to that rhythm., and ensure it consistently happens according to your chosen rhythm.

Blogs, webinars and seminars — there is a lot to be said and focused upon in order to get each of these to work at an optimal level, and it requires a book all for itself.

Blogs (written), podcasts (audio) or videos (visual) are all great ideas for weekly or biweekly content or tip sharing.

It is really important that you cover content which is not only interesting to you as an accountant (the latest budget announcements, the latest changes in taxation, etc.), but also, much more importantly, content that is interesting to your prospects (which means that it is completely okay, and advisable, for you to do a tip on marketing or sales generation or whatever it may be).

Webinars

Most of us have attended webinars at some point in the past. Generally, you register for a webinar. At the right time, you log onto the site and you get to hear the presenter and see their screen. Typically these will last anywhere from 45 minutes to 90 minutes.

We teach our Blackbelt Boardroom clients a very specific way to use webinars in order to get results (and again, it would require an entire book written on this subject to fully get how this works).

But even without comprehensive training on this topic, if you are doing it, even poorly, you are already doing something that your competitors are *not* doing. Which makes you stand out from the crowd!

The beauty of this is that it opens doors for you with people who want to find out more, but aren't yet ready to pick up the phone and call you — or, for whatever reason, simply may not be able to attend an actual live event with you.

Seminars

These typically take the most effort and money to get set up. But live seminar events are definitely the strongest method for connecting with your prospects, because they are live, face-to-face events.

As with everything else, there are ways to do this right. And there are ways to do this wrong.

The Funnel

From the above examples, it is noticeable that there is a funnel. New data enters your database.

John Doe. John then receives a weekly email/video-tip/blog/audio — anything, really — that gives him *great* content.

And he barely notices because his inbox is so full. In fact, he ignores most of your emails.

John has problems with his staff, and one day he sees that one of your blogs covers that specific subject. Because John is interested, he scans through your blog.

The content is good. He likes what he sees.

Next day it just so happens that John receives an email from you inviting him to your next webinar, which also happens to be on the topic of 'How to find the right staff in a tough environment.'

John is intrigued, so he registers for this webinar. Which he then attends a week later.

On the webinar you share some great content. He is engaged with you during the webinar and he actually likes you, your style and what he hears. Nothing there that puts him off.

And so the months go by.

During which John of course still receives your weekly blogs as well as your webinar invites.

One day, John receives a live seminar event invitation from you on another topic that is of interest to him. He remembers you from before and he thinks to himself, 'I'm free that day, why not?'

It just so happens that the week before the event, John meets up with his current accountant and suddenly discovers that there is a huge tax liability due which John had absolutely no awareness of before. It stings. Really sore. And John is in pain.

The day of the seminar arrives. The two of you are shaking hands in the seminar room and you start chatting. You hear about John's pains with his current accountant. And you explain to him how a lot of your clients have come to you for that exact reason — because at your practice with your super proactive processes and your dedicated client manager, you ensure that such things never, ever, ever happen.

There is a twinkle in John's eyes.

And a match made in Heaven is sealed.

The reality is that there are a lot of Johns out there. And these people are seeking one thing: answers. By continually putting great content out that provides insights, realisations, the start of solutions, ideas... there will come a point where our Johns simply can't ignore this content any further.

And that starts a relationship.

Once you have this process set up, the ultimate purpose of your marketing is to get a lot of interesting content out there so that people will be engaged enough to come to an actual live event with you. Which then becomes the ultimate conversion event. But at the same time, they could as easily convert during any of the steps of the funnel.

Do you as the business owner truly have enough time and energy to focus on making all the above happen?

I'm thinking *not*.

Which is exactly why having a marketing team on your side becomes vitally important.

For your practice, and for your freedom.

Adding New Data And Using Lead Magnets

One of the primary functions of our marketing is to continually be adding new data to our database.

We've got our weekly blogs, our webinars and our seminars going.

We are adding a whole lot of value to the world.

And we constantly want to be increasing our data.

This is where the use of lead magnets really comes in handy.

A lead magnet can take a number of different shapes. It could be a one-page checklist. It could be three pages of fun facts on X. It could be a short report on the five biggest mistakes that Y makes. It could be a book.

Its purpose? To serve as click bait.

Once your lead magnet has been created, you can advertise it in paid ads. We could approach an association of our niche clients (the plumbers' association, the dentists' association, etc.) and offer this great quality content to their members. You could mention it on LinkedIn or in an online group. In forums. You could place ads in magazines or trade association magazines, or it can be online. Pay-per-click advertising would take click-throughs to your lead magnet as opposed to offering to take them to your website's home page. Generally, your website's home page serves as a very weak landing page and is not the ideal place to send click-throughs to. You can pay for paid advertising (pay-per-click) on Google, Facebook and LinkedIn (each separately).

But the point is that in order for prospects to get hold of your bait, they have to give you their names and email addresses.

So normally a lead magnet will have a landing page of its own. In other words, 'Go to this xxx.com website to get your free report.' That directs them to a webpage which only refers to this one lead magnet, with space for them to insert their name and email address. Once they've done that, the lead magnet will be emailed to them.

Landing pages are easily created by your website person, or you can get templates such as the ones found here: www.leadpages.net.

Once you have their name and email address, they get added to your list, which then receives your blogs, your webinar invites and also your seminar invites.

Because you are constantly focused on putting really good content out there which they like and are impressed with, it will go a long way to warming such prospects up and positioning you as their #1 #2 (as referred to at the beginning of this chapter).

People who have downloaded your lead magnet have opted in, and until they unsubscribe they are happy to receive your great content.

It is possible to buy lists of email addresses and simply cold-blast your content to them, but this is generally considered spam and not the most ideal of ways to add people to your list.

To see an example of a lead magnet, go to www.accoa.co.uk/thehighlyprofitableaccountantworksheets

Telesales

If I received £1 for every time someone told me, 'I've tried it, but it hasn't worked,' I'd be able to retire very comfortably… today.

Telesales is a strategy. When done wrong, it does not work. When done correctly, it *does* work.

Firstly, let's take a look at who we could get to do telesales for us.

External telesales company:

Telesales is all these people do. You are a client of theirs. For a fee, they will arrange appointments for you. To find them, use Google. There are companies who do telesales purely for accountants which you could try out.

External full- or part-timer:

Someone is paid by you, probably on an hourly basis, to make calls from their home or their own base.

Internal full- or part-timer:

You have someone in your office who is *fully* — and *exclusively* — dedicated to this task.

In order to ensure that telesales fails miserably, follow these six steps:

Let's take a look at how you could ensure that your telesales campaign is a complete and utter flop — in other words, what *not* to do.

1. Set *no* criteria.
    'We don't specify what we are looking for. And then we complain when they pass us a lead of the single contractor who is earning £3,000 for the entire year.'

2. No accountability.
    'No, we haven't heard from the telesales company in the last two months. No, we're not going to call them... we're sure they'll come through at some point.'

3. No pressure.
    'We're nice, and we know they'll make it work some time...'

4. No sales process for cold leads.
    'Sales process? Well, I'll just rock up on their door at the appointed time and hope for the best. Yes, I know it will be a completely cold call, but what can I do?'

5. Pay for *booked* appointments.
    'They've booked me ten rubbish appointments and I've merrily paid for all of them.'

6. Wrong personality.
    The typical example here is when you get your very nice, and very gentle, receptionist in her 'spare time' to make some calls. That's like saying to a fish, 'Let's see how well you can climb that tree.' The fish simply wasn't built to climb trees.

Telesales success at last!

Now that we know exactly how to mess it up, let's take a look instead at how we get this to work really well for us.

Let's do the opposite of the above six steps.

1. Set clear criteria.
   'We only want prospects within X miles from our office who are turning over more than £X, and the person I wish to speak with is the Managing Director, or a Key Decision Maker.'

2. Accountability.
   'We are expecting weekly updated reports with results.'

3. Pressure.
   'We are expecting X amount of appointments within Y number of weeks, or we demand a refund/stopping the service.'

4. Excellent sales process for cold leads.
   Refer to the previous chapter on 'Sales for Accountants' where an excellent process is described step-by-step for you to follow. Without a process like that, you will walk into a very cold-selling situation which could be extremely unpleasant.

5. Pay for *kept* appointments.
   Sometimes telesales companies will book you weak appointments just to be able to tick the box on their side to say they have done their work. But it is quality you are after. And quality will actually keep appointments. So insist that you are only paying for kept appointments.

6. Right personality.
   Confident, strong, 'thick-skinned rhino' type. These people need to be able to withstand a lot of rejection and just keep going. Prior *outbound* calling experience is essential.

Once you have all of the 'weapons' as discussed in this chapter — and in this entire book — fully implemented, systemised and operational, you will find yourself at the helm of one of the strongest 'warships' on Planet Earth.

Are you going to do things that absolutely do not work? Yes.

Even with the knowledge base you now have, a lot of it is still going to be trial and error, sticking with it till you crack that nut.

But when you crack that nut, the sweet taste of honey awaits you on the other side.

4. Growth through Selling Other Services And Acquisitions

Jay Abraham, author of *Getting Everything You Can Out of All You've Got*, is a hugely wealthy and talented marketing guru. He said that the way to increase your sales is 1) increase the number of wallets that pay you money, or 2) increase the share of each wallet that pays you money.

Increasing the number of wallets clearly refers to new clients.

Increasing wallet share refers to providing your clients with additional services, for which in exchange they are happy to pay you more money.

Always remember that you already have an existing relationship of trust with your clients! And ultimately you and your firm's job is to look after your clients' financial welfare, not just their year-end accounts.

'Financial welfare'? What exactly does that entail?

Well, it would probably cover sections within each of these areas:

1. How can we help you improve your profits?
2. How can we help you grow your business?
3. How can we help you improve your cash flows?
4. How can we help you pay as little tax as possible?
5. How can we help protect you and your family in case of incapacity or death?
6. How can we help protect your assets through the right structures and insurances?
7. How can we help you eventually dispose of your business?

So the question to ask yourself is, 'Are we able to directly deliver those services?' *or* 'Do we have a contact we could put in touch with our clients to help them with that, from which we also receive a retainer.

Your script with your clients might go something along these lines:

'John, as your accountant, at the end of the day, I am interested in your full "financial welfare" picture. With that in mind, I'd like to set up a Navigator Meeting with you, where we want to cover a whole lot of bases to make sure you are actually properly covered for all eventualities. What does your diary look like for...?'

If they say, 'What is this about?' simply reassert the importance of this meeting and assure them that all their concerns and questions will be answered fully during the Navigator Meeting.

Perhaps you say, 'John, as a business owner there are a lot of things that can go right — and, more importantly, there are a lot of things that can go wrong. I want to do a Navigator Meeting with you to ensure everything is on the right track.'

When you get into the actual meeting, have a bit of an agenda with you. But the point of the meeting is to ask lots of questions. It is through asking a lot of questions that you will learn what they have, what is missing, and you will find that in a lot of cases, new additional work (directly offered by you or indirectly by third parties) *will* be uncovered — for which your clients would be very happy to pay.

Acquisitions

As a kid I loved riding my bicycle. In those days we had our BMXs and I could do all kinds of great tricks with mine. But I remember when I learnt to ride my very first bicycle. I was on a camping site with my parents. The moment came where they took off the stabilisers. I remember starting off, and suddenly the bicycle swerved really badly from one side to the other. But then I gained control... and just like that, for the rest of my life, I've been able to ride bicycles.

Today I can still get on any bicycle, and I can still ride it.

The same is true for your practice and your knowledge in running it.

Do I think that acquisitions of other accountancy practices should form a part of your future plans?

Most likely, yes.

Do I think that you should do this tomorrow?

My recommendation is that you first implement the things you've read so far in this book in your own practice. Therefore you learn how to ride the bicycle first. Get your own foundations right *before* you acquire another practice.

Personal experience says that if I'm building a skyscraper and my foundations are weak, at some point things are going to come tumbling down.

Rather, take a bit more time to get those foundations solidly in the ground. And then there will be more than enough time and opportunities to build on top of those foundations, far into the sky and towards your freedom.

Buying Retail Or Wholesale?

A few weeks ago I was looking for a bike rack for my car. I looked around and discovered that I could get a new bike rack at Halfords for around £180 — which is the retail price. I then had a look around eBay and Gumtree and eventually came across the exact same bike rack (only nine months old) for £60 — which is the wholesale price (okay... if you have to get technical, it *is* second hand, I agree... but go with the flow — there is a moral to this story).

If you go through a practice broker, you will end up standing in a queue of other purchasers. The broker and the vendor decide who in that queue they will eliminate. Even if you've put on your Sunday best, washed your hair and polished your boots, you could still very well be booted out with a look down their noses and a 'Thanks, but *no thanks.*'

And if you did manage to make it to the front of the queue, believe you me, the price you'd be paying for your investment would be the retail price.

How to pay the wholesale price? Potentially a longer journey, but...

You approach accountancy practices directly.

This could be through your own direct mail campaign followed up with telesales. And you persistently, even over a number of years, stay in touch with them until someone comes through, ready to retire, and because you've persistently been at the forefront of their mind, they approach you to start negotiations. And now you are not competing with 25 other purchasers.

How to Acquire an Accountancy Practice with No Money Down

Here is a story of one of my clients who is having a lot of fun. This client joined us a number of years ago on our Blackbelt Boardroom programme. And over a period of time he worked his way through every one of the steps described in this book and implemented it. This resulted in him making the jump from the SE step to the BO step and finally onto the I step.

Now that he is on the I step — that place where he has mastered how to ride the bicycle — he finds himself buying other practices. He's started playing *Monopoly* now. He has the money and more importantly, he has the time. But the best bit? He is buying practices with *none of his own money down*.

How does he do that?

In his own practice, he has built up an excellent track record for himself with the results he is achieving in his business.

He works hard on relationships.

He is constantly working on his communication and negotiation skills.

When he finds a practice that he wants to purchase (typically a retiring accountant), after his due diligence, he makes an offer to pay them 90% of the fee upfront.

He has an agreement with a certain bank that trusts him enough and is willing to lend him 90% of such deals. But then he also makes it a prerequisite that the vendor lends him the other 10%. And he will pay them that back over the next twelve months.

The vendor is happy — they have 90% of the money in their bank account within a few weeks.

The buyer is happy — the repayments of the 90% as well as the repayment of the 10% is all paid from the acquired practice's profits.

So the buyer has put zero of his own money into the deal.

Almost as if it were free...

And the buyer has...

Freedom.

Is this possible for you?

Who says it is not?

Having systematically and in a laser-focused way implemented the knowledge in this book, Phil found that he was finally able to put a tick next to each corner of our triangle. And when he looked back on his journey, he realised that he had indeed achieved the impossible. He had built a machine that gives him not only money, but also time.

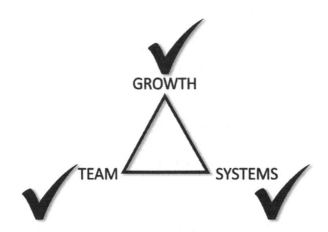

CONCLUSION

It was 3.15pm. Time for my call with David. David was now 51 years old. He'd had his practice for 15 years and they were turning over about £400k per annum. From our discussion, we concluded that David was probably spending most of his time on the SE step. Yes, getting to the I step sounded like a really great idea. And until we had our conversation, he had never quite seen it from that perspective. Up to that point in time, it was just work. He was slogging away every day on the treadmill.

But for the first time, probably ever, David could see a clear path — where he was and what he needed to implement to get himself onto the I step, and to freedom.

As both his kids were still under ten years old, it was quite an exciting vision for him to know that when he got himself towards the top end of the BO step, and then the I step, he would be able to have a lot more money as well as a lot more time available for himself and his family.

David realised that time doesn't stand still. Next year he would turn 52. The year after that, 53, and then 54. And he realised that if he didn't try something different, in a few years he could still very much be on the exact same treadmill as he was now.

Or, alternatively, he could possibly have put himself into a process which would have pushed him up that ladder... and into a place where he could choose freedom.

Either way, the time would pass.

He had to make a choice.

He could choose to do something.

Or nothing.

But David chose to send me an email at rudi@accoa.co.uk to arrange an initial quick twenty-minute telephone conversation to see if I could help him.

And right now, like David, you have a choice.

You see...

KNOWLEDGE

WITHOUT

IMPLEMENTATION

=

NOTHING

ZILCH

NADA

Yes... that is correct.

Knowledge Without Implementation = Nothing.

When you buy a book with the best ideas, you read it and then — with the best intentions in the world — you put it on your bookshelf for later and it gathers dust on your bookshelf.

Well, the truth is that you would probably have been better off *not* having read that book, because, as they say, ignorance is bliss.

Once you've read the book and you know that you've not implemented its teachings, then there is always this nagging part of your brain that keeps on reminding you forever and a day that you still haven't gotten around to it.

And the only way to eventually lay that little voice to rest is to actually take action.

And do something.

The client I mentioned towards the end of the previous chapter who is now playing *Monopoly* and buying other practices with none of his own money? When he joined our programme, he was very much on the SE step. Eighteen months later, through the process of implementation that we use to get our clients to implement the knowledge in this book one step at a time, this client had qualified with his black belt.

And now that he is on the I step... he's mastered how to ride the bicycle. He has a body of knowledge that will stand him in very good stead for the rest of his life.

He has freedom.

Or there is Mark: when Mark started with us, he was already well onto the BO step. Mark is 67 years old and not particularly interested in the I step, as such. But what he wanted was to be able to retire very comfortably, yet still be involved with his practice. With the systems we've put in place, he is now working only three days a week in his practice, which for him is very comfortable. He is focused on working only with clients that he chooses to work with and doing work that he chooses to do.

He has freedom.

Or there is Carl: Carl is in his late 50s. And as much as he says he doesn't want to, Carl is a workaholic. He loves it. Every moment of it. And because he's made the jump onto the I step, with more than enough money and time on his hands, he is an avid real-life *Monopoly* player, actively buying other accountancy practices, other businesses, both within the UK and overseas. He is a true entrepreneur.

He has freedom.

And Phil?

Phil has moved up the Freedom Ladder from 'Self-Employed' to 'Business Owner' and all the way to 'Investor'. He's put a tick next to each corner on our Team-Systems-Growth triangle, and made it *ding!*

His practice is now run by his very capable management team. He also has a team member who actively helps him hunt for and then acquire failing businesses. Between them they have the know-how on how to turn failing businesses around.

Phil spends a lot of time in the Mediterranean with his family on their yacht. He now has more money than he has ever had. He has his time back, which he cherishes very highly. And Phil is truly loving his life.

At the end of the day, the job of your business is to provide you with the lifestyle that you choose. Once you've decided what lifestyle you wish to live, then starts the hard slog of changing your business around.

But that hard slog only lasts for a relatively short while.

And then you will be set free.

To live the life of your dreams.

Freedom is your birth right!

Demand it!

And make it happen.

NEXT STEPS

The knowledge in this book really can give you your freedom.

If that is what you want.

Of course you could implement this by yourself. And if that is your choice, I honestly do wish you all the best of luck!

But if you feel you need further guidance...

If you've read this far and you're wondering how we might be able to help you get all these steps implemented, one step at a time as we have done with countless other practices, then there are some ideas on the following pages.

WANT SOME HELP?

If you feel stuck and frustrated with where you are at, and you are absolutely serious about making changes *right now*, then why not arrange your complimentary twenty-minute Practice Growth Audit.

During the call you will:

- Discover the essential blueprint for growing *your* practice fast.

- Find out the #1 thing that's currently holding you back (and how to get round it).

- Identify the most powerful actions that will move you forwards to the place you want to be.

The purpose of the Practice Growth Audit is to troubleshoot your current situation and to determine if I can help you.

If I can then we'll arrange another call to figure out how. If I can't, then I'll try and point you in the right direction.

Please note — this call is only available for practices whose turnover is greater than £150,000 per annum.

If your current turnover is less than £150,000 per annum please see the following page for additional resources that could help you.

To book your complimentary twenty-minute Practice Growth Audit go to www.accoa.co.uk/session.

Take that next step towards your own freedom.

ADDITIONAL RESOURCES

If you ever get stuck implementing the concepts in the book and need some extra help, we have a variety of additional resources to help you on your way:

- **Blog:** on a weekly basis we post short, actionable content to our blog in the form of videos, written articles and downloadable content. To find out more go to www.accoa.co.uk/blog.

- **Online Training Session:** in order to get the most out of the ideas and concepts in this book, you can also access a bonus online training. Register for free at www.accoa.co.uk/thehighlyprofitableaccountanttraining.

- **Downloadable Guides & Cheatsheets:** here are some of our most popular downloadable guides and cheatsheets that you can implement immediately to see results.

  - The Referrals Maximiser – The 3 Step System That Signs A-Grade Clients
    www.accoa.co.uk/referrals-maximiser
  - The Outsourcing Cheatsheet – The 3 Step Process To Mastering Outsourcing
    www.accoa.co.uk/outsourcing-cheatsheet
  - 33 Ways To Increase Your Client Retention
    www.accoa.co.uk/33-ways-to-increase-client-retention
  - The 5 Biggest Mistakes Partners In Practice Make (and how to avoid them)
    www.accoa.co.uk/5mistakes

THE HIGHLY PROFITABLE ACCOUNTANT SEMINAR

As a special thank you, I would like to offer you two free tickets to any of our upcoming seminars.

These events are a great opportunity for you and your senior team to spend time working ON your business and start building the practice that you want.

During the seminar you will:

- Deep dive on the 3 keys to predictable practice growth and how to leverage these to increase your profits annually
- Learn the in-depth process for finding and developing a self-reliant team that allows you to work less
- Uncover the step-by-step method for creating systems that work without you
- Learn exactly what's working now (and what's not) in other accountancy practices from around the country
- Leave the event with a clear roadmap showing exactly what you need to do in order to create the practice that you want

Tickets for these events are usually £147 per person and I have included two for you free of charge.

I like to get to know each of my attendees individually and keep the seminars as interactive as possible which is why there is a maximum of 40 seats for each event.

In order to claim your two free tickets, and to find out more information about our upcoming events, please go to www.accoa.co.uk/thehighlyprofitableaccountantseminar and complete the short form.

I look forward to seeing you at one of our events in the future.

READY TO HANG UP YOUR BOOTS?

Perhaps you've read this book, but because of where you are in your life, you really can't be asked to make the changes – and you are ready to move onto the next phase of your life.

If you are thinking about it, or you are ready to sell your practice, the asset you've spent years of your life building, chances are very good that I might be able to connect you with someone who is looking to acquire your practice. Get in touch with me. I might be able to help you.

You can reach me on
rudi@accoa.co.uk.